NEW

Neighborhoods

The Consumer's Guide to
Condominium, Co-Op, and HOA Living

Gary A. Poliakoff and Ryan Poliakoff

EMERALD
BOOK CO.

Published by Emerald Book Company, Austin, TX, www.emeraldbookcompany.com

Distributed by Emerald Book Company

For ordering information or special discounts for bulk purchases, please contact Emerald Book Company at PO Box 91869, Austin, TX 78709, 512.891.6100.

Design and composition by Greenleaf Book Group LLC
Cover design by Greenleaf Book Group LLC
Illustrations by David Whamond, Three In A Box, Inc.

Publisher's Cataloging-in-Publication Data (Prepared by The Donohue Group, Inc.)

Poliakoff, Gary A.
   New neighborhoods : the consumer's guide to condominium, co-op, and
HOA living / Gary A. Poliakoff and Ryan Poliakoff ; [illustrations by David
Whamond]. -- 1st ed.

   p : ill. ; cm.

   Includes bibliographical references and index.
   ISBN: 978-1-934572-18-4

1. Condominium associations--Law and legislation--United States--Popular works.
2. Condominium associations--United States--Popular works. 3. Housing,
Cooperative--Law and legislation--United States--Popular works. 4. Housing,
Cooperative--United States--Popular works. 5. Homeowners' associations--Law and
legislation--United States--Popular works. 6. Homeowners' associations--United
States--Popular works. I. Poliakoff, Ryan. II. Whamond, Dave. III. Title.

HD7287.67.U5 P655 2009
333.33/8   2009927330

Part of the Tree Neutral™ program, which offsets the number of trees consumed in the production and printing of this book by taking proactive steps, such as planting trees in direct proportion to the number of trees used: www.treeneutral.com   TreeNeutral

Printed in the United States of America on acid-free paper

09 10 11 12 13 14   10 9 8 7 6 5 4 3 2 1

First Edition

This book is dedicated to our families,
for their constant love and support.

This book is about New Neighborhoods —the many thousands of communities where owner associations govern the lives of millions of people. These neighborhoods could not operate without the selfless contribution of the volunteers who serve as directors and committee members, the professionals who manage and operate the properties, and the owners, who give up certain traditional homeowner rights for the good of their communities. This book was written for all of these people.

No book is written alone, and we would like to especially acknowledge and thank Carmen Sierra, Tina Siregar, JoAnn Burnett, Michelle Soler, Debra Lewin and Howard Shapiro for their insight and encouragement.

CONTENTS

FOREWORD

Shared ownership communities in the United States have a long and checkered past. Condominiums, cooperatives, and planned communities have been introduced and developed in phases throughout history. In fact, planned communities in the United States were first introduced in the 1820s. With improved transportation and an abundance of land and resources, the first "streetcar suburbs" were developed around the major cities on the East Coast. Then, with the rise and expansion of the railroads over the years, the population became mobile, following jobs and family all over the country, taking with them a need for flexible and creative housing solutions. The concept of the cooperative arrived from Europe around 1900, and condominiums were created in larger numbers after 1961, when modifications to housing law empowered the Federal Housing Administration.

Today, shared ownership communities come in all shapes, sizes, heights, and configurations, including condominiums, condominium hotels, time-shares, cooperatives, homeowner and property owner associations, master associations, dockominiums, manufactured housing parks, office park condominiums, and various combinations of these. All shared ownership communities, however, share certain obligations:

1. A set of governing documents creates both rights and responsibilities, through the use of covenants and restrictions.
2. Owners of lots or units automatically become members of the community association when they buy a home or lot. ·
3. Every owner is required to pay assessments to cover the cost of maintaining, repairing, and replacing the common property areas and of operating the association.
4. Every owner has an undivided ownership interest in the property.

Shared ownership communities continue to be constructed in ever-growing numbers, as cities and counties have discovered the benefit of leaving the issue of infrastructure for the new communities to the developers. In 2008, according to the Community Associations Institute (www.caionline.org), more than 60 million people across the nation were living in approximately 300,800 common interest ownership communities. Meanwhile, more than 1.7 million people served on association boards, and the associations themselves had annual operating revenues of more than $41 billion.

But the structural components of many of our buildings are aging. Maintaining and repairing the common elements and common areas is a costly proposition. In addition, hurricanes and other storms, floods, fires, and so on have contributed to an insurance crisis for community associations. Given the current realities of the economy, including the loss of jobs, foreclosures, gasoline prices, etc., boards of directors struggle not only with the idea of whether to fund reserve accounts, but also with the collection of ordinary maintenance assessments to pay operating expenses.

Our system of community regulation is aging, too. The governing documents for many associations were written in the late 1960s or early 1970s, and given the extensive lifestyle and legislative changes since those times, these documents may no longer be adequate (or even legal and proper) to deal with the issues raised by compliance and enforcement.

In my experience, the biggest challenge to successful operation of community associations is the lack of education among the consumers who are buying homes and units within these communities, and sometimes among the volunteers who serve as directors of the associations. There are very few courses available on a local level to help a buyer understand just what he is purchasing and how the community association works. What are his rights? What are his responsibilities? How will he fit into the scheme and development of his new community?

Where can a buyer go to get an explanation of the sometimes arcane complexities of community association operations and regulations—an explanation that can be understood by the average person who doesn't have a law degree?

I'm happy to report that the resource for which we have been waiting rests now within your hands. This is a book by experts in community association practice, written in plain English for the layperson. At last, there is a comprehensive presentation of all the varying aspects of community association living, with real-life examples and featuring a mix of insights and humor, in which a potential buyer can find an education on what he is really buying and what he can expect, and a director can get some guidance on her responsibilities and obligations in the realm of governance.

Reading what the Poliakoffs have written is a great way to start and then enjoy your journey as a denizen of a common interest ownership community—and to encourage your participation in the process.

Ellen Hirsch de Haan, J.D.
President
Foundation for Community Association Research
Alexandria, Virginia

INTRODUCTION

The first time Murray Candib heard the helicopter circling around his condominium, he probably looked for the hidden cameras. After all, how many times have *you* been interrupted during dinner by the distinctive *thwat, thwat, thwat* of helicopter blades spinning above your kitchen table? The second time this happened, Candib must have felt extremely put upon; ten or twenty times later, he was understandably irate.

Candib's upstairs neighbor in his luxury Miami condo, Palm Bay Towers, had developed a habit of landing his helicopter wherever he pleased, including on and around the property. For many weeks, Candib and his family were battered by the roar and thud of a several-ton machine setting down outside their window. Candib sued, but it took a trial and an appeal before a judge was finally willing to rule that helicopter landings are potentially bothersome enough that they constitute a *nuisance*.[1] In finally finding for Candib, the appellate judge wrote:

> [I]nherent in the condominium concept is the principle that to promote the health, happiness, and peace of mind of the majority of the unit owners since they are living in such close proximity and using facilities in common, each unit owner must give up a certain degree of freedom of choice which he might otherwise enjoy in separate, privately owned property. Condominium unit owners comprise a little democratic sub society, of necessity more restrictive as it pertains to use of condominium property than may be existent outside the condominium organization.

So out of anarchy came utopia—a basic, discrete explanation of the theory behind all forms of commonly owned property, whether they are planned developments, condominiums, or cooperatives. Because you own property in common with your neighbors, you inherently give up certain rights that are considered sacrosanct by traditional (detached) homeowners. The time-honored principle of "my house, my rules" goes out the window when you share your walls, floors, and ceilings with two or three other people, all of whom want their own rules applied. And make no mistake: Nothing creates hard feelings more than sharing property with others.

It has been estimated that nearly sixty million people in the United States live in *shared ownership communities (SOCs)*, each

---

1. A legal term describing an act that interferes with the quiet enjoyment of your home—more on this in Chapter 11.

governed by a mandatory membership association, or *community association*—so this book is for just about everyone. Long gone are the days of communes and shtetls. And yet a large majority of Americans are still influenced by a complex and largely misunderstood system of ownership, in which people are forced to give up some of their autonomy to benefit the greater good of their neighbors.

The purpose of this book is to explain the workings of these communities—these "New Neighborhoods"—to the people who live in them, and to let new purchasers know just what they're getting into. While there's a lot of law involved, we've done our best to keep things as simple as possible. Each chapter is informative yet, we hope, entertaining as well. A number of subjects that we cover are relevant to different topics and so are discussed more than once; for example, we address rules and regulations with the explanation of your documents in Chapter 4, but we also dedicate Chapter 10 entirely to this topic. You'll hear crazy stories that may remind you of your neighbors—or may make you realize and appreciate how great your neighbors really are. We'll describe your rights and responsibilities, as well as those of the association, and show you exactly why some of these crazy rules were written in the first place.

It has often been said that a man's home is his castle. For many of us, this couldn't be further from the truth.

LET'S START AT THE VERY BEGINNING
(AN INTRODUCTION TO SHARED OWNERSHIP COMMUNITIES)

We begin this book with a basic assumption: If you're like the vast majority of readers, when you purchase your residence you are primarily concerned with its physical features, not with whether it is a condominium, a cooperative, a planned development governed by a community association, or some other form of shared ownership community. The important thing is that it's your home. Home is a powerful concept. It conjures up images of food and family, of celebrations and tragedies. Your memories live there along with you; you may have raised children in your home or entertained grandchildren there. A home affords you privacy and sanctuary from an often difficult, complex world. Home is where you go to *escape* your problems, not to collect new ones.

And yet the reality can differ dramatically from this idealistic notion, depending upon individual circumstances. Many people, especially those living in impoverished communities, live in large family units that occupy increasingly shrinking amounts of space. In some areas of the world, families are afforded virtually *no* privacy of any kind. Often extended family units of a dozen or more members live in the same house, sharing expenses in an effort to make ends meet. On the other hand, Americans enjoy perhaps the highest standard of living in the developed world, and the issues that arise in a typical community are often far less critical than the global question of basic subsistence. That, however, does not invalidate these issues.

People have lived in shared communities for many hundreds of centuries. As far back as the Stone Age, extended family units or villages might share a single fire pit. The ancient Romans, especially the poorer citizens, had collective baths, gardens, temples, and sanctuaries. In the 1800s, the Napoleonic Code, which evolved in France, endorsed and legitimized the condominium concept, which was also later recognized under English common law. But perhaps the most modern of premodern housing concepts were the pueblos of the southwestern Native Americans, specifically the Taos Pueblo.[1]

The Taos Pueblo ("Taos" rhymes with "house," not "chaos") is a Native American community built in the mid 1300s in what is now New Mexico. The old village, which is still standing and occupied, is a World Heritage Site, sharing company with the pyramids of Egypt, the Vatican, and the Great Wall of China.

---

1 The majority of our research on the Taos Pueblo comes from John J. Bodine's excellent resource, *Taos Pueblo: A Walk Through Time.*

The Taos Pueblo is frequently referred to as the "oldest inhabited apartment house" or even the "first condominium." Certainly, it was never an actual condominium, but the design of the Pueblo, as well as the lifestyle of the Taos Indians who live there, share a surprising amount in common with modern SOCs.

The Pueblo structure itself has multiple stories, with as many as five apartments stacked one on top of the other. Access to the upper floors is by ladder; this was done for obvious security reasons, and today some modern doorways have been added on the lower floors. Each apartment consists of two rooms: one for living and sleeping, and one for cooking, eating, and storage. Each home is independent of the others, and none are connected by internal passageways.

These private, family living areas are separate from a number of shared, outdoor community elements, including beehive ovens, drying racks, and kivas (chambers used for ceremonial religious rituals). The river that runs next to the Pueblo is used for drinking and cooking water for all the inhabitants. The Taos people have also built churches and cemeteries for the use of the community.

So we know that the Taos Pueblo features owned elements, such as the actual apartments, and common elements, like the ovens and drying racks. A guiding principle of the Taos people is that they should always "move evenly together"—that the individual should always bow to the community. Every resident of the Pueblo is expected to contribute to the upkeep of the property, whether through cleaning, cooking, or serving in the local government.

Is any of this starting to sound familiar? Like the Taos, SOCs rely on member involvement to govern and maintain the property (though the maintenance element is more often than not handled through financial assessments rather than manpower). All owners have their own private living space, but they also share certain common property, such as barbeque grills, pools, gardens, and gyms. The concept has been updated, certainly, but is not that far removed from the lives these Native Americans have lived for hundreds of years.

This raises an obvious question: How has a lifestyle practiced for hundreds of years found favor in modern times and in fact become widespread? Perhaps it comes down to basic economics, a principle that will likely never change. It is less expensive for five families to maintain a comfortable lifestyle than it is for a single family. Gardening, maintenance, upkeep, repair, and improvements cost money, and it is more palatable to share these expenses with a number of neighbors than to carry the burden on one's own. Fifty years ago it might have been reasonable for an average family to have a home with a reasonably sized backyard, maybe even a small pool and a playset for the kids. But the pressures of growing populations, coupled with dwindling reserves of land and an increase in the relative cost of living, have forced families into sharing "personal" amenities that were once considered standard accessories of the American dream.

Of course, sharing leads to inevitable dilemmas. Imagine that you and your best friend were to buy a house together. How would you maintain it? Would you have a housekeeper clean every day? Every week? Which repairs would you let slide, and which would you fix immediately? If the TV broke, would you replace it or simply buy some more books? Remember, we're talking about your best friend—the person most likely to share your interests and values—so some of these questions will practically answer themselves, though there are still bound to be disputes. Now imagine the situation in a typical SOC: You are basically buying a house with three hundred families whom you have never met, and with whom you may or may not share similar values. Those questions are no longer as easy to answer.

In reality, these issues aren't all that different from those that we face in our own government. Do we go to war or fight for peace?

How much do we spend to feed the hungry? Do we provide universal health care? What laws do we pass? How do we punish those who refuse to follow them? Humans have spent thousands of years developing alternative systems for dealing with these questions, and the system that Americans rely on, democracy, has been proven to be the gold standard.

So perhaps it's easiest to think of a community association (the "government" for an SOC) as a private democracy. We'll even use that in our working definition:

> *community association. n.* a private democracy designed to govern the inevitable questions that arise as a function of group ownership

Until the 1960s (at least in the United States), there were only a handful of "condominiums" in existence (although, as we mentioned, the general concept dates back hundreds of years). And while basic SOCs have existed for more than a century, planned developments did not become popular until the 1960s either. Both are constructs of law and politics, bred by necessity. They are regulatory rocks carved by the slow trickle of thousands of legal entanglements. The concept of the *modern* SOC is the result of decades of trial, error, and refinement.

Before we get into the specific types of SOCs, let's take a moment to discuss the time-honored notion that a man's home is his castle. This idea represents the widely held belief that property owners have carte blanche to do whatever they want with their own homes and their own property, whether they choose to leave that property in disrepair or polish it like a South African diamond.

However, in the courtroom this idea does not translate into such simple terms. Judges understand that a man's home is not always his castle, and that sometimes the good of a community outweighs the rights of the individual. What follows is perhaps the most venerable quote in all of property law:

> Every man may justly consider his home his castle and himself as the king thereof; nonetheless his sovereign fiat to use his property as he pleases must yield, at least in degree, where ownership is in common or cooperation with others.

This quote is attributed to a Florida judge in the famous Sterling Village case, which involved a condominium. The principle, however, is genuinely universal, and it really relates to the overall classic concept of libertarianism: Do no harm to others, and do whatever you want to yourself. Essentially, rules in SOCs are designed to ensure that even the wackiest neighbor has little chance of disturbing the community or acting as a lead weight on property values.

So if you bought your home assuming that it was your castle—that you finally had your own personal fiefdom, your piece of the autonomous American dream—you should probably rewind a bit and realize that, unless you live out in the sticks, no man's home is his castle. Apparently, it does in fact take a village.

Now that we know *why* SOCs exist, *who* first came up with the idea, and *how* they came to be, it's time to discuss *what* the different types of communities are and how each type is differentiated from the others.

PLANNED DEVELOPMENTS GOVERNED BY A MANDATORY MEMBERSHIP ASSOCIATION

Let's accept at the outset that you've probably never used the term *planned development governed by a mandatory membership association*—yet it's likely that the majority of you live in one, or you wouldn't be reading this book. In a planned development, the developer purchases a bare plot of land and subdivides it into neighborhoods, sometimes including amenities such as a golf course, a clubhouse, a gated entry, and utility access areas. He then files his development plan with the local governmental authority. This master plan has its own set of *covenants, conditions, and restrictions (CC&Rs)* that govern the entire property; you can think of these simply as the various rules that residents have to follow. But within this community might be a number of separate associations that control the individual neighborhoods, including condominium associations, cooperatives, and the most common form of SOC government, the *homeowner's association (HOA)*.

In fact, HOAs are so prevalent that the term has become a generalized way to describe any SOC that consists of houses or townhouses, whether or not they are governed by an actual homeowner's association (as opposed to a condominium association or a cooperative). Remember, however, that an HOA is a type of community *government*—not the type of community itself. Still, rather than speak of planned developments—or *planned urban developments (PUDs)* as they may be called in Northern states—the general public continues to use phrases like "I live in an HOA"—and in this book, sometimes we will, too.

Nearly all modern suburban neighborhoods are planned developments, governed by some combination of mandatory membership associations (usually HOAs). Twenty years ago your home and your neighbors' homes were nothing more than marks on a map in a developer's office. The *developer* (the person who owns the land and plans the development) hired civil engineers, architects, and planners to artfully divide the acres of property into, say, 450 single-family homes and townhouses spread around a fill-dredged lake. You can't see it at eye level, but viewed from above, the road system looks vaguely like a spider web—so they decided to call the community Silk Pointe. (Notice that every truly luxurious community uses "ye olde English" spelling conventions—the more *e*'s at the end of the word, the more likely it is that you'll overpay for your property.) The association itself owns the "everyman's land," such as the roads, the park, the gatehouse, and the lake.

In an HOA, unlike a condominium or a cooperative, homeowners generally own their land and the house itself—that is, the walls, floors, ceilings, etc. However, the CC&Rs often control specific elements of how your home appears—perhaps the color of paint you use, the type of landscaping, or the roofing shingles. These are all prime examples of restrictions on the rights that are traditionally granted to homeowners—again quashing the "Your home is your castle" concept. Some associations are quite lax, while some are extremely rigid and their rules may even have the unintended effect of creating an unappealing, aesthetically bland community with the character of an army barracks. It is incumbent upon the rules writers and the architectural committees to strike a balance between control and flexibility that has the desired effect of enhancing the community rather than stifling it. Keep in mind that the purpose of these rules is not to create hardship for homeowners; it's to ensure that you don't have to look at your neighbor's re-creation of the gingerbread house from *Hansel and Gretel*. The direct influence, in addition to preserving your eyesight, is to stabilize and potentially raise the overall property value of the community by ensuring that all the homes are architecturally and aesthetically consistent.

As in all SOCs, the rules that govern your HOA are found in two places: your state laws (either a proprietary statute or some version of the Uniform Common Interest Ownership Act—more on these in Chapter 5) and your *declaration of covenants, conditions, and restrictions*. This declaration (also referred to as the *documents*) is your bible—you should have gotten a copy when you bought your home, and if you didn't, then make sure you get one now. It contains all the rules and regulations that you and your neighbors are required to follow, and it lays out the rights and responsibilities of the association and the homeowners. Get one, read it, then read it again. In any SOC, your life is controlled largely by these two sets of rules—the laws and the documents. It's in your best interests to become familiar with them.

Now, when there's a dispute between the association and the homeowners, or between individual homeowners themselves, who enforces these rules? For that, you need to check with your state government. Some states have established an agency with full regulatory control over condominiums or HOAs, or both. For states that have no such agency, the majority of disputes are handled through the court system.

CONDOMINIUMS

While probably not the most prevalent of our examples, the condominium is certainly the most venerable—the spiritual granddaddy of all SOCs. It is also widely misunderstood. Historically, the condominium is the second principal attempt (cooperatives being the first) to create an ownership situation in a multiresidence building, usually one where units share walls, pipes, and wires (i.e., an apartment building). Today's condos have expanded past the traditional high-rise building; for example, two halves of a townhome may together form a single condominium, as may marinas, hotels, RV parks, and parking garages. But high-rise buildings are where they got their start.

So how did the creators of this concept get around the fact that your ceiling is your neighbor's floor, and that your bedroom wall is also your neighbor's living room wall? The solution is very creative but also esoteric, at least to nonlawyers. In a condominium, instead of owning the physical building you essentially own the air within it. You own a box of air the size of your unit, bordered by exterior walls that may or may not be shared. More specifically, you own everything from the inner surface of the perimeter walls inward, and from the inside of the ceiling to the top surface of the floor. You don't own the walls themselves, but you own all the airspace inside the walls.

Actually, that's not entirely correct, because you do own the walls—just not by yourself. In a condominium, every owner owns an undivided interest in the shared areas of the property, which are generally referred to as *common elements* or *common areas*. This interest is *appurtenant* to the unit. Let's define those words, because they're important—and probably entirely unintelligible to anyone but the most ardent condo commando. You own an *undivided* interest—essentially, you own the entire building, together with every other owner. You don't own a fiftieth of the building, as you might assume; you can't put your hands on that one section of wall and mark it as your own. Think of it this way: You don't own a part of the building. Instead, you and the other residents own the whole building. And *appurtenant* (the accent is on the "pur," as with the word *impertinence*) simply means that your share in the common elements "goes with" the unit. So every owner owns an *undivided* interest that is *appurtenant* to the unit: It can't be divided or sold separately. Whoever owns the unit owns the undivided share of the rest of the property. Got it? Now you're a certified lawyer.

In an HOA, you own your house: They're *your* pipes, *your* insulation, *your* walls, *your* lawn. But a condo is a totally different beast. Everything inside the walls—the pipes, the wires, the fluffy pink stuff—is generally owned by the unit owners in concert. (Check your documents to be sure: In some documents and statutes, any pipe that services only a single unit is the sole responsibility of that unit owner.) That means if a pipe is leaking inside "your" wall, everybody pays to fix it. That also means if a pipe is leaking inside your neighbor's wall, you're on the hook for your fair share. Payback's a bitch.

But what specifically determines who owns what? Does your unit just end where the walls end? Actually, it's not that simple. The unit boundaries are determined by (drum roll, please) . . . the documents! Your documents (which you've read by now, right?) generally lay out what you own individually and what everyone owns collectively. The documents also specify what you're responsible for fixing and what the association must repair.

This is a good time to clear up another misconception. In a traditional condominium, unlike in a planned community, the association doesn't usually own anything. That is, it's not accurate to say that you own the airspace and the association owns the common elements. The association is, as we discussed earlier, a mandatory membership government whose members consist of every owner of a unit in the building. The association manages and governs the building, and it is responsible for maintaining most of the common elements—but it does not *own* the common elements. As members of the association, you and your neighbors each own an undivided interest in the common elements. (There are exceptions to this rule, and associations *can* own property. But we'll discuss that later, in Chapter 3.)

Think of it this way: You and three friends buy a Corvette convertible. You all own the car together. You decide that decisions concerning the car will be made by democratic vote of all the members of a micro association, the Four Friends Corvette Convertible Association, the members of which are . . . the four of you! You then elect Bill as the president of the association; with three kids and a wife who won't let him out of the house, he's clearly the most responsible. Bill makes most of the decisions concerning how the car is maintained and how it is used. But neither he nor your association *owns* the car outright. The four of you own the car together, and the car is operated and maintained by the association. So nobody owns anything—and everyone owns everything.

Now, what rules govern how the association runs the condominium? The documents and the state laws (or *statutes*). Again, each state is different. In Florida, look to Section 718 of the Florida Statutes (the Condo Act). In Texas, it's Title 7, Chapter 81 (for pre-1994 condominiums) or Chapter 82, Texas's version of the Uniform Condominium Act (for post-1994 condos). In Illinois, it's 765 ILCS (Illinois Compiled Statutes) 605—the Condominium Property Act. Are you a New Yorker? Look to RPL (Real Property Law) 339, the New York Condominium Act. Westward ho? Californians can rely on Civil Code section 1350—the Davis-Stirling Common Interest Development Act. Or you may reside in one of the twenty-five states that have passed some version of either the Uniform Common Interest Ownership Act or the Uniform Condominium Act.

Remember that, at least as a matter of common law (the body of laws that has been passed down by judges presiding over centuries of cases), there is no such thing as a condominium. The idea of "air ownership" was created through laws passed by our various state legislatures as a solution to the problem of joint high-rise ownership. And it's actually a very creative solution.

I know what you're thinking: "Damn. Are you telling me I just paid a quarter of a million dollars for *air*?" No—you paid a quarter of a million dollars for air *and* for an undivided interest in all the stuff that surrounds the air. But you may be far better off than the folks who own shares in the next form of common interest ownership: the cooperative.

COOPERATIVES

Today, except in big urban areas (like New York City), cooperatives are not widely found. They are arguably the least favorable form of common interest ownership for the homeowner. They are tough to finance, frowned upon by banks, and difficult to *alienate* (transfer or sell).

In a planned, single-family residential development, you own your land and anything on it, and the association owns all the other areas that are either titled to the HOA or dedicated to the homeowners' common use. In a condo, you own the space where your unit sits, as well as an undivided interest in the common elements. In both situations, you are a property owner. The quality of your ownership is called *fee simple* title—the highest form of property title that you can own. You have the actual title—hopefully stored somewhere safe.

In a cooperative, on the other hand, the building and all the common areas are owned by a corporation. You simply own a piece of that corporation—some number of corporate shares. That's it. You don't actually own property at all. You do not have the rights generally afforded to property owners, such as unrestricted alienation. You just own shares in a corporation that owns a very large investment.

And therein lies the problem. A bank can't give you a mortgage to buy a unit in a co-op, because you're not buying a piece of property. It can give you a bank loan to buy the shares in the corporation that owns the building, but most banks require far more stringent credit checks and more money down for these loans than for property ownership.

Why? Mainly because you may not be able to recoup the bank's money if you need to sell your shares. See, you own only a piece of a corporation, and the corporation has broad powers to prevent you from transferring that piece if the directors don't like the new prospective owner. In most states, a condominium association or HOA has little or no power to prevent you from selling your unit or house. It may have a right of first refusal, but that would simply mean that it could buy the property from you to prevent the sale to your proposed buyer. But in a co-op, the board can simply reject the prospective buyer, telling you that you can't sell your unit to that person. This is a gigantic problem in the property law world. Being able to alienate your property is one of the prime rights of property ownership; co-op owners give up this very fundamental privilege.

There's another concern. With other forms of SOCs, members own their property individually, so it is financed individually. If your neighbor can't pay the mortgage, the bank will own the property (after foreclosing on it) and will eventually sell it to someone else. You are not responsible for covering any of those costs.[2] But in a co-op, the corporation owns all the units and all the land. If a single unit owner defaults on his or her loan or refuses to pay for maintenance, it is the responsibility of the corporation to make up the difference. That means you're on the hook for your neighbor's apartment, and that's why co-ops are so careful about whom they allow to join the association. Any person who is not financially solvent could potentially default, leaving the payments to the rest of the members. For this reason, co-ops generally require that prospective new residents provide the admissions committee with several years of tax returns and bank statements as well as numerous character references—none of which are typically required by a condominium or HOA.

So why buy into a co-op? In truth, there are very few good reasons. In New York City, where many buildings predate the legal creation of the condominium concept, the only common ownership system available was a cooperative, so that's what you'll find there. Some co-ops have been converted to condominiums, but most have not.

---

2 That said, even in a condominium, if the homeowner is forced into either foreclosure or bankruptcy, the association may be responsible for a portion of the unpaid maintenance. In some states, a foreclosing bank *is* responsible for paying maintenance (up to a certain amount), but in others they are not responsible at all. If your state lets banks off the hook, then make sure that your association is pursuing late payments to the full extent allowed by the law.

That means if you're looking for an apartment in Manhattan, you may have no other options (but if you do, a condo is the way to go). However, a small percentage of potential buyers actually *like* the fact that their building will be able to exclude "undesirable" applicants.[3] But either way, when choosing a home, you should presume that it's always better to be a homeowner than a shareholder.

MULTICONDOMINIUM ASSOCIATIONS AND MASTER ASSOCIATIONS

You might think that each building in a development must have its own membership association, but that's not entirely true —there exists such a beast as the *multicondominium association*. In the multicondominium association, a single association is responsible for the maintenance of multiple buildings, each of which exists as a separate condominium within a single planned development. Most maintain separate books and records for each individual condominium and a separate budget for shared common expenses. Be aware if this type of association governs your new home, because it can add a lot of politics and infighting to the job of community management.

A multicondominium project can also be governed by individual condominium associations, while using a single *master association* to manage the elements that are common to the entire development. Take, for example, a typical development project of multiple highrises. One way of designing that project would be for every owner in every tower to own the entire property together as a single entity; it would simply be a condominium with several different buildings. The problem, of course, is that multiple buildings will double or triple the costs of maintenance for owners, as they must pay not only

---

3 Some of the "undesirable" applicants who have been rejected by a co-op include Andy Warhol, Richard Nixon, Mariah Carey, Carly Simon, and Madonna. So if you're rejected, take heart—you're in good company.

to maintain the other towers, but also to staff them with their own housekeepers, groundskeepers, valet, and front desk staff. Many developers, therefore, set up these projects as individual condominiums that are linked together by a separate master association. Each individual condominium is able to create its own rules and regulations governing use of its own common elements, and make its own determinations as to budgeting and services. However, a master association manages any elements shared among the condominium buildings (typically community property such as pools, tennis courts, and common grounds); all the condominium owners are responsible for contributing funds to this master association, too.

So is this type of structure beneficial or detrimental? Certainly, there are both pros and cons. The biggest con relates to a popular saying: "Too many cooks spoil the broth." When one board of directors controls a single development, that board can make decisions that are consistent for all owners, who can rest assured that their board (whether or not they agree with its actions) is the only entity responsible for the most important investment they're likely ever to make. With separately declared condominiums, each governed by its own association, not only do you run the risk that the operations of two different buildings can vary in significant ways, but you also have to rely on a third association to manage the shared amenities over which your board would otherwise have direct control—a cumbersome and expensive arrangement.

Consider this situation: The owners of condominium A, Tower Pointe One, are old-guard octogenarian condo commandos, tight with their checkbooks and willing to forgo as many services as possible to afford their quiet retirement (which more often than not involves only the four walls of their units). Condominium B, Tower Pointe Two, was built ten years after the first condo was completed, and it is filled with young professional couples and recent retirees looking for an active luxury lifestyle. The owners at Tower Pointe Two love the pool and the tennis courts, and because they spend so much time out of their units, they want the grounds kept spotlessly.

By now, a couple of things should be obvious. The owners at Tower Pointe One and Tower Pointe Two hate each other. They have entirely different needs and expect totally different things out of their respective associations. As far as their individual towers are concerned, that's not much of an issue. But what about the shared common elements, such as the pool and tennis facilities? These areas are governed by a master association made up of members of both towers, all of whom may vote for the master association board. Of course, the Tower Pointe One homebodies are far more active in the master association than the Tower Pointe Two yuppies, who have other workaday responsibilities outside their homes, so it has been run since its inception by the eightysomethings. Tower Pointe Two residents want to add towel services and a juice bar—but the master association has no interest in upgrading the pool area, which half of the residents rarely use. In fact, the elder residents recently voted to stop heating the pool, since that service was never promised in the original documents and it costs a fortune.

Are you getting some sense of the kind of angst that this structure can engender? In some condominiums, the members of the various associations have been feuding for decades without find ing a way to come to a compromise, either on their own individual associations or on governance of the master association. As a result, nothing gets done, and the buildings have fallen into a shameful condition of disrepair.

The point is, before you buy into any multicondominium community, it's best to get the lay of the land and see how everyone gets along—because this will have a very real and direct effect on your lifestyle and your overall enjoyment of your home.

For some of you, it may be too late to mention the obvious, but it must be said: Owning property in an SOC is not the right choice for every buyer. This is especially true for condominiums and co-ops. First, you will be living in very close proximity to your neighbors. Smells, noises, and disturbances are common. Some are inevitable and are actually not correctable—they are just part of living very close to other people. Also, regardless of the type of SOC, there are elements of your life over which you will have no control. The way your balcony looks, for example . . . whether you keep pets . . . the type of flooring that you install . . . how often you cut your lawn . . . whether your children are allowed to play in the pool. Very basic life choices are often controlled by the rules of the association, because those choices have the potential to affect your neighbors and to infringe on the quiet enjoyment of *their* property.

Think carefully. Are you the type of person who can't stand the smell of Chinese food? Does cigarette smoke make you retch? Do you wake up at even the smallest noise? If so, stay away from condos and co-ops, at the very least. Are you the type of person who hates when other people tell you what to do? Who believes that when it's your house, it's your rules? If so, you should stay away from SOCs entirely. Because in the New Neighborhoods, it's not always about your house or your rules.

We'll end the chapter with an example of a very successful SOC: Paradise Lakes in Land O' Lakes, Florida (yes, like the butter). Paradise Lakes is a gated community with twenty-four-hour security, two heated pools, two hot tubs, three sand volleyball courts, a restaurant, a café, a massage salon, a nightclub, three bars, five tennis courts, and an exercise room. It's beautiful, bucolic, and peaceful—and maybe it sounds perfect for you. Just one thing (did we forget to mention?): Clothing is optional. Actually, total nudity is preferred. That's right: Paradise Lakes is a long-standing, successful nudist condominium. And the owners love it that way.

The point is that not every community, no matter how perfect it looks, is right for every buyer. Make sure you do your homework and read the documents before you buy. A well-educated buyer will never be embarrassed later on.

THE BIG, BAD WOLF
(THE ROLE OF THE DEVELOPER)

If there's a universal truth among shared ownership communities, it's that every owner grows to hate and fear the meanest, evilest villain on the planet: the developer. Reviled for his shoddy construction! Cursed for failing to build a second tennis court! Despised for his long, pointy tail and sharpened pitchfork!

In reality, you'll find that developers are just like all businesspeople—some are trustworthy, and some are not. Some take pride in their work, and some don't. Either way, there are a host of laws and regulations in place to govern the responsibilities and liabilities of the businesses that worked for years to plan and build your new home.

First, let's stop a moment to consider the word *developer*. Who is the developer of your SOC? Is it the person who conceived of the project? Or maybe the architect who designed the buildings? Perhaps it's the construction company that actually built the homes, or the financier who invested his cash. Maybe it's some combination of any or all of the above. This is just a way of pointing out that *developer* (sometimes *seller* or *sponsor*) is actually a loose term used by lawyers to describe the person who assumes liability for a project and who is responsible for development and any express or implied warranties. This entity can be different for every project, so people can't assume that they know who the developer is just because they bought their unit from a common sales office. There will always be one or more entities that have legal responsibility for the effective completion of the design and physical structures of your particular community, and this is the person whom you will learn to love to hate.

A developer's responsibilities and liabilities vary by state, but some basic rules are universally applied. First, the developer has the responsibility to build a structure and facilities that are substantially similar to those promised in one of various written guarantees, usually a sales contract, property report, and/or prospectus. Second, the developer is required by law to provide a warranty of varying length to cover defects in the property caused by faulty construction or design. Following are descriptions of each of these two safeguards.

PROPERTY REPORTS

In 1968, the U.S. Congress passed ILSA—the Interstate Land Sales Full Disclosure Act. Administered by the Department of Housing and Urban Development (HUD), ILSA establishes a complex set of rules intended to protect buyers of property, including units in SOCs. Following are the highlights of the act.

Under ILSA, any developer who plans a community is required by law to file what is known as a *property report*. A property report contains a number of documents and disclosures that include, among other things, proof of clean title to the property, as well as a detailed description of the units, their boundaries, and any planned recreational facilities. It also includes a detailed summary of the CC&Rs that will govern the planned development. The developer must give the property report to every purchaser of a new unit prior to the buyers signing a contract or agreement to buy a unit in an SOC.

There are, however, two common exceptions to the ILSA filing requirement. First, if a project is smaller than one hundred units, a property report is not needed. Second, a developer may unconditionally agree to complete construction within two years, thereby exempting himself from the filing requirements; if the developer misses the two-year window, however, every buyer would then be permitted to cancel his or her contract. But even with these two exemptions in place, the vast majority of developer projects still require the filing of a property report.

In addition to ILSA, many states require their own analogous document, sometimes called a *prospectus*, to be filed by developers of even smaller projects. It is not uncommon for prospective buyers to receive both a federally mandated property report and a state-mandated prospectus for the same development.

The property report comes with a catch: If a developer alters a project after filing a property report, and if that alteration renders the original report false in any way, the original contracts may be cancelled. So the property report, while largely protecting developers, also gives buyers the ability to rescind their contract if the project should change.

That said, this basic right of rescission must be taken in concert with a legal principle called the *statute of frauds*. The problem addressed by this doctrine is the ageless issue of oral misrepresentation. Consider this example: A buyer walks into the sales office for a new development—Swaying Golden Palms on Ocean Pointe. She is greeted by Barry Wolf, a sales representative for the developer. His job is to move units by any means necessary. So he shows the buyer a sample of a unit, maybe a piece of a bathroom or kitchen, and then begins his spiel—the sales pitch. He talks of lavish luxury, the kind once enjoyed by kings and dignitaries. Acres of tennis courts . . . a full-service spa with primeval mud baths . . . pet massage . . . perennially unobstructed views. Mr. Wolf is "puffing up" his promises to make the units more attractive, and in fact this kind of oral misrepresentation is often referred to as *puffery*. Most ordinary people call it "lying"; nonetheless, it's a very common practice in the real estate world.

The buyer thinks she's buying into a once-in-a-lifetime opportunity—a building that will rival Saddam Hussein's palaces for sheer opulence. She signs a contract without bothering to read it and awaits her new home in the sky. Fast-forward two years. Our buyer finally closes on her unit, only to find that many of the promises were never fulfilled. There's only one tennis court, and it's smaller than regulation. There is no spa in sight, and in fact she finds that her beloved dog, Daisy, is not even allowed in the building. What's worse, her view of the ocean is directly blocked by a water tower installed by the city after the project broke ground. She feels cheated and wants to sue.

This brings up a troublesome issue of law: How can claimants (the people who file a lawsuit) prove that they were damaged by an oral misrepresentation? It always comes down to the word of one party against the other, and it's almost impossible to prove who is telling the truth. Mr. Wolf will insist that he never promised any of those things—only said that they were planned or perhaps just being considered, or never mentioned them at all. This basic question of fact is a problem in any lawsuit.

The solution developed by the court system is to insist that all contracts for the sale of land (as well as all contracts over a certain time period or dollar amount) must be in writing to be enforceable, and that no oral representations will be considered part of the contract. That is, a buyer can never rely on the word of the seller— only on what is written on paper. If buyers understood this common rule—the statute of frauds—it would solve a lot of problems. Let the developer's crony spout his lies—if the promise is not in the prospectus or the contract of sale, it can't be relied upon.

Unfortunately, most nonlawyers are both unaware of this law and generally trusting of other people; they don't realize that they shouldn't rely upon promises made by overeager real estate agents and slippery developers. They hear the promises, believe the lies, buy the property without ever looking at a prospectus, and are disappointed when the eventual reality does not meet the beautiful fantasy.

The statute of frauds is a very important legal principle that bears repeating: If the promise isn't in writing, it doesn't exist. Your property report, prospectus, and contract exist for a reason—they are legal documents that apprise you of the exact structure that the developer is obligated to build. If a promised element is not in those documents, you can assume that it will never see the light of day. If you follow this simple rule, you will never, ever get burned. *Believe what you see and not what you hear.*

What if the developer doesn't live up to these written obligations? The prospective buyer has two options: Rescind the purchase contract before the closing (give up the house) and demand the return of the deposit, or close on the property and then sue to collect damages from the developer for any difference in value (or to force the developer to comply with his promises). We'll talk more about the second option later.

WARRANTIES

The second line of protection afforded to owners is through warranties. Everyone should be familiar with the concept—you probably have a warranty on your car, your television, even your refrigerator. The seller of the product *warrants* (promises) that what you've bought will not break for a certain amount of time after it is purchased—otherwise it will be replaced.

While today they are taken for granted, historically there were no warranties attached to the sale of real estate. Instead, buyers were expected to rely on the ancient concept of caveat emptor: "Let the buyer beware." Fortunately, most states have now recognized that caveat emptor is outdated and have passed a series of laws that provide statutory warranties for all buyers. In doing so, our government has implicitly acknowledged that, for the average family, a home purchase is one of the most important transactions of a lifetime, and that families deserve to be protected against construction fraud and misdealing.

As a general rule, there are three types of warranties applicable to the purchase of a new home in an SOC: express, implied, and statutory.

Express warranties are simply written promises made by a developer, in which it agrees to be responsible for repairs to the building for a certain period of time.

Implied warranties of fitness and merchantability are general warranties that are implied by law, based on the simple fact that the developer has built a building intended for a specific purpose (in this case, residential housing). The law imposes an obligation that the building be free from defective materials and constructed in accordance with applicable building codes, construction practices, and engineering standards.

And last, *statutory warranties* are warranties of either type (typically borrowed from the common law) that have been codified into the state statute—and can therefore be used in any SOC (barring a disclaimer in the documents).

Owners can use each of these warranties to force the developer to live up to its responsibilities and provide a fit, habitable residence.

But what if your building is twenty years old, and the board has just discovered that the original roof is defective and about to collapse? This situation raises a legal issue called the *statute of limitations*. Ordinarily, the court system requires that claimants who wish to bring actions against those who have harmed them must do so within a reasonable amount of time after the damage was discovered. This ensures that any further damage is minimized, and that the responsible party is made aware of the defect before the cause has been long forgotten, so that any findings of fact can be made while there are still facts to find. That means you can't ignore your roof until it collapses and then run screaming to the builder. Instead, the law specifies that an action must be brought by the harmed party after a defect is known or *reasonably should have been known*. That is, if the defect would have been discovered through ordinary inspection and maintenance, you ignore it at your own peril.

The actual period covered by the statute of limitations (the amount of time you have to file a lawsuit) varies by state, as well as by the legal theory used by the particular attorney. Here's what you should know about the coverage period:

- Under the common law passed down by the courts, warranty lawsuits must be filed within four years of the date the defect was discovered (or, in the exercise of reasonable diligence, should have been discovered).

- Under the general umbrella of the Uniform Act, warranty lawsuits must be filed within six years, or the opportunity is lost. That is, if seven years after taking over the building from the developer it becomes apparent that the air conditioner is a lemon, you're out of luck.
- To add to the confusion, several states have a "savings provision" in their laws that *tolls* (delays the expiration of) the statute of limitations until after control of the building transitions from the developer to the unit owners. That is, if the developer built a condominium in 2005 but didn't turn over the building until 2007, the statute of limitations clock would not begin to tick until after the turnover (essentially giving the owners an extra two years to identify potential problems).
- It is also important to distinguish between warranty periods and statutes of limitations. A warranty against construction defects generally begins when the project has been given a certificate of occupancy; this date may very well be before a single resident has moved in. The statute of limitations, however, will not begin to run until turnover (which can sometimes be years later). So it is quite possible for a community to sue the developer long after any warranties have expired, because the harmed party's right to sue is still recognized.

Obviously, all this puts a tremendous amount of pressure on the owners of any new project to bring in experts who will scour the property for any potential problems. Which brings us to our next issue . . .

TRANSITION AND TURNOVER

At some point, any purchased product needs to leave the hands of the seller and enter the care of the buyer. For most items, that time comes when the product is bagged at the store, or perhaps when it is delivered to your home.

In an SOC, however, the developer is essentially selling hundreds of individual items that are all interconnected by a certain percentage of shared items and are purchased at different times. So when exactly does this turnover occur? And if any units remain unsold, what prevents the developer from holding onto control of the association indefinitely?

The terms *transition* and *turnover* refer to the point in the evolution of an SOC when the right to control the association's board of directors passes from the developer to the unit owners. It's best to imagine this timetable as a sliding scale, with total developer control on one side and total unit-owner control on the other. At first, the developer owns all the property and every unit, and therefore has the right to control the association. In fact, a prerequisite to building any SOC is the establishment of some form of government—whether it is a community association or a trust (less common, but still an option in some states)—to manage the association property. Initially the developer will control this government and will have the right to appoint the entire board of directors. All this occurs before a single unit has been sold.

Then an important event occurs: the first closing. Bonnie Homebuyer walks into the sales office with a gaggle of attorneys and a mass of complicated documents, and she hands the developer a mint in money for a small piece of the SOC and an inalienable right of membership in the association. She is now our first nondeveloper association member.

Of course, the vote of a single homeowner is insufficient to gain any say over the operation of the community, so Bonnie must wait until enough units are transferred to buyers for a majority to be reached, at which point the nondeveloper homeowners would have the power to elect their own board of directors (essentially ousting the developer).

But what happens if the developer is a little pokey in his sales? Bonnie could be stuck living in an empty, forgotten building with an insolvent developer running the show.

To prevent just such an occurrence, the law provides owners with several protections to ensure that the developer ultimately turns over the development and its association to the rightful owners. The law varies slightly by state, but the Uniform Common Interest Ownership Act provides that developer control of the building must terminate either sixty days following the transfer of 75 percent of the units, two years after the developer has ceased to offer units for sale in the ordinary course of business, or two years after any right to add units to the project has been exercised—whichever occurs first. So, eventually, the developer will have to surrender his baby to its new parents.

In reality, the main problem is not one of a developer who won't let go, but more commonly of owners who won't grab hold. It is not at all uncommon that the owners of a new SOC fail either to vote in an election or to put their names forward for consideration as candidates for the board of directors. In this situation the developer will petition the court to appoint a receiver who will manage the property (at a cost to the unit owners, of course) until the owners are willing to accept their responsibilities. Or the developer may simply resign from the board and walk away from the project, leaving it up to the unit owners to sort it all out.

Assume for the moment that your building's units have all been sold and are fully occupied, the developer has surrendered the board, and the officers have been elected. Before anything else, the board should hire an engineer, a lawyer, and an accountant (see more about accountants in Chapter 9). In fact, several courts have stated that hiring an engineer is a legal responsibility of any such board.[1] As we mentioned earlier, it is the duty of an association to identify defects within a reasonable amount of time; that's where the engineer (or engineering firm) comes into play. Your engineer will do a full review of the buildings and property owned by the association and will then write a detailed report that specifies which elements were not built in accordance with the approved plans, accepted practices of good workmanship, or applicable building codes. Once complete, the engineering report becomes a management tool that will help the association's superintendent to schedule maintenance and repairs; it also will help to resolve questions of defective construction among the developer, architect, engineer, contractors, and manufacturing suppliers.

The association should also hire a lawyer—not because of the imminence of any lawsuits, but rather to help the association navigate a multitude of turnover issues, including not only negotiations with the developer but also unit owner issues, collection of maintenance fees, violations of rules and regulations, and the basic, everyday legal questions that arise from the management of any corporation.

Be prepared for sticker shock, however; between your engineer and your attorney, any large association can expect to spend tens of thousands of dollars, and much more if it is ultimately necessary to litigate. However, this is a very small figure compared to the cost of repairing millions of dollars in undiscovered defects—all of which, ultimately, will be borne by the entire ownership.

---

1 In a concurring opinion in the 1987 *Conquistador* case, Judge Glickstein wrote, "This case, in my view, points up the necessity that condominium associations, as soon as the unit owners take over control, engage professional engineers or architects to determine whether the buyers received all that they thought they had bought. The likelihood is remote that volunteer unit-owner directors, however well meaning, can ascertain as well as trained experts can whether the development buildings have structural integrity."

RESOLVING DISPUTES

Imagine, then, that your association has been turned over, the new board is in control, and you've hired an engineer and a lawyer. Your engineer will provide you with an engineering report that details any problems with the construction, whether minor or major. It will note, for example, if the developer forgot to paint the pipes or failed to put a drain in the pool. In addition to these defects, you will likely have your own "wish list" of items that you feel the developer promised but never provided. When you add everything up, you're going to have a total cost to correct the mistakes and repair the property. This number is very important, because it will determine whether the alleged defects are minor and easily corrected by the association, or whether the cost-benefit analysis justifies pursuing a lawsuit against the developer.

Invariably, when it comes to the engineering report and other demands, there will be points of contention between the owners and the developer. The owners' complaints may be exaggerated, over-blown, and overreaching. The developer, in contrast, will argue that many of the problems are actually the result of improper mainte-nance of the building by the unit owners and the association. And so it goes, for many months: claims and counterclaims, endless meet-ings and courtroom briefs. Often, how these matters get settled has more to do with the negotiating skills and patience of the parties than with the actual facts involved.

This process is going to bring up a simple fact of human nature: Nobody likes to be taken advantage of. We expect to get exactly what we pay for, in perfect condition. But still, some people can take this drive for perfection to an unreasonable level. All of us have friends or family members who inspect their purchases with a mag-nifying glass and who insist that every product entering their home must arrive in mint condition, without flaw. These are generally very unhappy, nervous people—the same people whom you always think twice about inviting to your dinner party.

If you live in a typical SOC, the basic law of averages says that some of your fellow owners are exactly this type of person—and they are going to be barking for the developer's blood. Perhaps your neighbor's living-room window has a wobble that can be seen between 3:00 p.m. and 5:00 p.m. when you view it at an exact 35-degree angle. Maybe the light fixture in the master closet is a half inch closer to the right wall than to the left wall, or the balcony railing is a centimeter higher on one side. Some owners will present the developer with three or four pages of punch-list complaints, "defects" that probably will never be fixed to their satisfaction.

This brings us to our first rule for any SOC owner, particularly if you are an aspiring or a current board member: You will never make *everyone* in the building happy. Honestly, there are just some people who are naturally unhappy; they will never be satisfied, no matter what repairs or improvements are made. You're never going to change them.

In any event, remember that a building is, at its most basic level, a completely handmade piece of functional artwork, often built by the lowest bidder using construction workers with fairly limited artisan-level experience. If you've ever bought a new car, you know that the chances of a flawless vehicle are extremely low—usually there's an idiot light on the fritz, or maybe the window sticks a bit. After all, a car is a huge feat of engineering, and it's built at least partly by hand. No one reasonably expects a car to come out of the factory like a perfect little Frisbee.

Yet for some reason, despite the fact that an SOC is infinitely more complex than any vehicle, and that the buildings are built entirely by hand, people expect their homes to be perfect. This is just not reasonable. Your goal should be to have a home that is functional, safe, and visibly well constructed, at least from a reasonable distance. But if you're inspecting your new home with a microscope, you can rest assured that you will find problems—and no one, no matter how well trained, will ever fix those issues to your satisfaction.

So the goal of any prudent board of directors is to determine what actual and significant flaws exist within the property, and how much money it will take to repair them. After this determination is made, it's time to investigate the three main methods of dispute resolution: mediation, arbitration, and litigation.

Of course, there is one form of dispute resolution that should always be pursued first: good-faith negotiations with the developer. Not all developers are evil, sadistic villains. Many of the responsible, trustworthy ones realize that satisfied buyers will be the best sales force for their next project.

Failing such efforts to reach an agreement, however, *mediation* is the mellowest and least costly form of dispute resolution. The involved parties get together with a *mediator*, a person trained to negotiate disputes. Everyone presents their wants and needs, and the mediator attempts to help the parties come to a compromise. (Note that *every* solution will be a compromise. Don't ever assume that when you present your engineering report and wish list the developer will smile and throw another million dollars into the property.) Neither party is bound by the mediator's suggestions, so it is up to the owners and the developer to reach a reasonable resolution. Still, in situations where the developer's responsibilities are minor, mediation is a relatively inexpensive method of resolving your differences.

The next step up the ladder is *arbitration*. In arbitration, a private party (usually an independent lawyer or an off-duty judge) acts in a quasi-judicial role, hearing evidence from the parties and then making his or her own determination of an appropriate settlement. Arbitration can either be binding or nonbinding, as well as voluntary or involuntary, depending on the requirements of the individual state and the agreements signed by both parties. Arbitration is more costly than mediation, and it will usually require you to hire some form of legal counsel; however, it is far less expensive than the granddaddy of dispute resolution—litigation.

Litigation is the big enchilada. It's the subject of dozens of popular courtroom dramas, and it's what everyone thinks of when they imagine a typical courtroom. However, 99 percent of all litigations never reach a courtroom—it is far more cost-effective to settle disputes out of court rather than invoke the enormous expense of a full trial. And we mean *enormous*: It is not uncommon for a typical lawsuit to cost each party six or seven figures.

Litigation begins when one party files a lawsuit against the other party in an appropriate court (usually a state trial court). There are very specific rules that govern *discovery* (the sharing of information between the parties) and how the trial will move forward. In the interim, both parties will scramble desperately in an attempt to settle the lawsuit before the ultimate trial date.

This fact is often confusing to typical SOC residents, who have seen lawsuits glamorized on television so frequently that they pine for the glory of an unmitigated victory. But part of managing a condominium involves making sound business decisions, and litigation is very rarely a sound fiscal decision.

Consider the following. You have purchased a unit in a new SOC. After all the reports are filed, you estimate that your $100 million condominium requires $1 million in necessary repairs (a typical moderate number for a project of that size). The developer quickly offers the owners a settlement of $500,000 so that it can walk away from the project. "Outrageous!" the residents cry. "Half of what we deserve? Sue the bastard!"

So the board, under pressure from the owners—who are eager to secure their recovery and restore their honor—hires an attorney and files a lawsuit against the developer. The court system flows like molasses, of course—you can expect a typical lawsuit to take years to resolve. Some states (Florida, for example) have strict notice laws that require the building to give the developer a certain amount of time (usually several months) to correct as many issues as it wishes before a lawsuit can even be filed. Such laws mitigate against clogging the court system with a flood of lawsuits, by forcing both sides to cool off before going to court. The thinking is that if the parties attempt to communicate first about the claims and whether they can be remediated, the action might be avoided entirely. In reality, however, this cooling-off period may simply tack on even more time before the dispute can be resolved.

A year or two of hard-core litigation could easily cost residents half a million dollars in legal fees, which are not generally recoverable in construction litigation. So even if you win the lawsuit, and even if you get 100 percent recovery (which almost never happens), you're still right back where you started—netting $500,000 for your building. Yet it's two years later, and the building has been in disrepair while you've been waiting for the judgment.

There is another significant risk element involved in the pursuit of a full trial. Most communities are built by limited liability corporations that retain very few assets after turnover, and a judgment against those corporations could essentially be uncollectible. So the unit owners could find themselves half a million dollars in the hole, with a worthless judgment against a nominal corporation.

This fact is foreign to almost all nonlawyers, but it's the reason that any good lawyer will tell you that he or she rarely (if ever) goes to trial. It's a simple calculation: Trials are not cost-effective! They are a last-ditch solution used only with totally recalcitrant developers.

This is not to say that you shouldn't ever sue the developer. In fact, lawsuits are common. It may be necessary to file a lawsuit for the sole purpose of tolling the statute of limitations. But most of these lawsuits will be settled long before you ever see the inside of a courtroom, and that's a good thing. That's good business management and good lawyering.

Still, it doesn't satisfy the bloodlust, so you can bet that there will always be a small contingent of owners who don't want to be made whole—they want vengeance. They want to show the world the evil developer's true colors. And to achieve this goal, no cost is too great. Hopefully none of these owners are on the board of directors. But if they are, watch your wallet—it's going to get lighter, and for no good reason. The smart, prudent board (like any good business owner) will calculate its desired recovery against the costs of various dispute resolution options and will pick the strategy that makes the most business sense. That may or may not include a lawsuit, but you should be thankful if it doesn't.

So we've discussed the role of the developer—the person or entity who has legal responsibility for the construction of your community. In building the property, the developer will have granted owners multiple warranties, which may be enforced either through negotiation, by means of nonbinding dispute resolution, or in the court system. But in the meantime, you've just bought a building— or at least part of one. What exactly did you buy, and what are your responsibilities? This is the subject of our next chapter.

3 YOU GET WHAT YOU GET AND YOU DON'T GET UPSET
(BUILDING BLOCKS OF OWNERSHIP)

The most massive of entities—our universe—is made up of tiny atoms. Even our own lives can be sorted into individual parts—family, career, personal. Shared ownership communities are no different: As with other things, it's easier to understand your investment if you break it down into the individual building blocks that define its essential character.

COMMON INTEREST OWNERSHIP

At their most basic level, all SOCs represent some form of common interest ownership—that is, all owners, directly or indirectly, collectively own some aspects of the community. As we discussed in Chapter 1, that share can either be undivided, as is the case with a condominium; divided into shares, as is the case with a cooperative; or owned by the community association or the master association. This concept is crucial to the SOC structure; it means that you are responsible for your piece of both the assets and the liabilities of the community. A tropical storm wipes out the clubhouse? Guess who gets to pay a portion of the repair costs. The condo lobby is blackened by fire? Either get out your wallets or break out the sponges. This structure is almost totally unique in American residential home ownership. It's most similar to a partnership or a grouped investment opportunity (like a corporation or a mutual fund), though in any corporation the owners are protected somewhat by limits on the amount of money they would ever have to put into the investment. In common interest ownership housing, every owner will ultimately be responsible for both the good times and the bad times, with very little financial flexibility.

In coastal states, owners may wonder whether they will be stuck with a "special assessment" of funds in the aftermath of a hurricane. Many are surprised to hear that the answer is *yes*—100 percent of the time. Deductibles for windstorm insurance typically run 3 percent of the total coverage, which can amount to millions of dollars. More often than not, all the initial repair costs must come out of the individual owners' pockets. If you buy a condo, and the seller tells you that you don't have to worry about special assessments, he is lying to you. Any emergency or unbudgeted repair in any SOC will often require the association to raise funds from the owners. That's part of the cost of doing business, and it's a basic reality of shared ownership.

When you own a home, you get to make choices about the timing and cost of any repairs that you pursue. For example, if your upstairs toilet leaks and stains the ceiling below, you may choose to save $500 and just leave the stain for a while (who ever really looks up at the ceiling, anyway?). But in an SOC, the association has the legal duty to maintain the property essentially in like-new condition, whatever the cost. If the board of directors chooses not to repair the property, it is violating its duty to the members of the association. So it will always choose to make the repair—and if cash is short, the board will bill you. That's the downside. The upside, of course, is that when split five hundred ways, a $500 repair costs you only a dollar. Economy of scale, but very little individual flexibility—those are the hallmarks of an SOC.

THE UNIT

In any community, your primary ownership interest (and the largest portion of your investment) will be your home, also known as your *unit*. A unit is a single piece of an SOC that is individually owned (or, in the case of a cooperative, that confers exclusive-use rights) and over which you have the largest amount of autonomy.

In an HOA, your unit includes your home, certainly, plus your driveway and probably even your yard. There's perhaps a fifty-fifty chance that you also own the sidewalk from your home to the next tract, while the street and sidewalk in front of your home are definitely either common property or public property. Still, living in an HOA-governed SOC undoubtedly feels the most like living in any other neighborhood—your unit is pretty clearly defined to your home and your property, and you have a lot of autonomy over how that space can be used.

For condominiums, this division gets a bit trickier. Traditionally, most people assume that the boundaries of a condominium unit are the insides of the vertical and horizontal walls. That is, your unit includes the air bounded by the walls, floors, and ceilings. However, the items inside the walls (such as pipes and ductwork) may or may not be part of your unit, depending on the definitions in your documents. So if you don't own the walls, who does? You and everyone else, collectively.

A cooperative, as we described in Chapter 2, is a totally different ball of wax; it's the only type of unit that you don't actually own. Instead, the entire building (including the walls, pipes, ducts, wires, roof, insulation—everything, really) is owned by a corporation, and you own one or more shares of that corporation. As owner of those shares, you are given the right to use your particular apartment, but you don't really own it, at least not outright. Your *shares* would be the piece of the corporation that you own.

Regardless of the type of SOC, exactly what you *do* own—the vertical and horizontal boundaries of your unit and, in a condo, whether you own any elements within the walls—will be defined in the documents. But it's important to read your documents and determine what you own by yourself and what you own collectively, for a very basic reason: If you own it, it's more than likely that you're responsible for its maintenance and repair. You may assume that a leaking pipe in the wall isn't your problem, but if the documents say you own that pipe, and if it damages the unit underneath you, it's going to become your problem very quickly. You have a duty to maintain your own unit in a manner that prevents damage to the common elements and to other units. Don't assume that because you can't see it, it's not your concern.

But the main reason to become familiar with the boundaries of your unit is because this is the only area that you are allowed to use by yourself, to the complete exclusion of the other owners. You may not be able to keep the wacky septuagenarian who wears a thong bikini from lying out at the pool, but you can certainly keep her out of your home.

Now, that doesn't mean you can operate a methamphetamine lab in your kitchen without repercussions. Laws still apply in your unit, just as they would in any home. More than that, most states (and most documents) give the association unfettered access to your unit to make common repairs and prevent damage to the common elements. So think of your unit as a teenager's bedroom—off limits, but with parental privileges.

COMMON ELEMENTS

What about everything else? Nearly every other building, wall, tree, and piece of grass in your SOC is either a *common element*, a *common area*, or *association property* (for a more detailed discussion of these three categories, and the association's duty regarding their maintenance, see Chapter 8). A common element is condominium property owned collectively by the unit owners and available for their common use. As we explained before, in a condominium you don't own a *piece* of each common element—you own the whole thing (together with everyone else). Although it's a bit esoteric, this concept is important because it's the main reason that you generally can't exclude other owners from the common areas. (Exceptions to this would be ballrooms and clubhouses, which sometimes allow reservations in exchange for an "exclusive use" fee. That is, you are paying some sum of money for the privilege of excluding your neighbors from their own property for a limited period of time.) Typical common elements might be the roof, the exterior walls of the building, the parking lot and garage, the pool, the tennis court, the clubroom, the billiard room, the media center, the gym, the spa or sauna, and the lobby—anywhere that's outside the units but within the boundaries of the SOC. Common elements also would include landscaping, sidewalks, generators, elevators—any property outside the unit boundaries.

Because common elements are owned by everyone, everyone generally gets to use them whenever they want. Still, the association can pass appropriate rules governing the use of the common elements, including time-of-day restrictions and reservations (such as for tennis courts), as well as basic rules and covenants that govern conduct within the common areas. You may own it, but that doesn't mean you have carte blanche to do whatever you desire. Barring restrictions that might flout state or federal law (such as prohibiting wheelchairs on the pool deck), the association is able to restrict your use far more than if it were a private home or even part of your unit. If the association says no music at the pool, than there's no music at the pool. If it decides beach balls must be smaller than 10 inches, that's the way it goes. The common elements are one of the few purchases you will make in your life over which you have very limited control (other than through active participation in the association, which we get to in Chapter 6).

LIMITED COMMON ELEMENTS

By now you may have realized that there are a number of "gray area" elements—they would seem to be part of your unit but aren't within the defined unit boundaries. Your balcony or patio would be a prime example. It's technically not part of your unit, but that doesn't mean you have to let everyone use it, right? Probably. More than likely, your balcony is what's referred to as a *limited common element*.

Limited common elements are elements owned collectively by the members of the association, but with exclusive-use rights granted to an individual unit owner; this "limited" access lends the term its name. Balconies are a classic limited common element (though this can vary by association, so check your documents); other examples include parking spaces, vestibules, and some rooftop areas (bordering a penthouse, for example). Any exclusive-use area of the property could potentially have been defined as a limited common element instead; this determination depends solely on state law or, in its absence, the association documents.

So why does it matter? Why not just include the balcony within your unit boundary, as some documents might? The primary reason is one of control—it's easier for an association to regulate how you use your balcony (which can be seen by other unit owners) than how you use your own unit. Also, this designation potentially shifts responsibility for major repairs from the unit onto the association— though most of the time you'll find that your documents assign you the responsibility for upkeep of limited common elements, such as regular painting or replacement of broken glass.

Essentially, a limited common element is a common element with an air of exclusion. You don't own it, but you have the right to keep the other owners out. So go out on your balcony and beat your chest—you're entitled to do so.

ASSOCIATION PROPERTY

This next category is truly abhorrent to a lot of owners in SOCs (particularly in condominiums), who feel strongly that the association should never be in the business of owning real estate. Still, it is sometimes necessary and appropriate for the association to hold the actual title to *real property* (land and buildings, or *real estate*— as opposed to money, jewelry, cars, clothing, etc.) for the use of all residents. In fact, in the case of HOAs, association property is the de facto standard.

Remember, the association is essentially a corporation of which every owner is a member. You are a member of the corporation, and the corporation governs and maintains the property. With *association property*, the corporation itself owns one or more elements for the use of the entire community, either having purchased these elements using money collected through assessments or having been deeded the property at the time of turnover (as happens in nearly every planned development). The difference here is largely one of legalese—the corporation, rather than the individual members, owns the property. You will still be responsible for maintenance payments to maintain the elements, but those also might include financing charges to cover the purchase costs.

One classic example of *acquired* association property would be a clubhouse that was built after the community was developed; another would be several extra parcels of nearby land that were purchased either for extra parking or to control view rights. Any property that the members of the association wish to own after the initial development would have to be purchased directly through the association and would therefore become association property. As a unit owner, you still have the responsibility to maintain it, and you can still use it—you just don't own it.

APPURTENANCES TO THE UNIT

There's that funny word again—the one that doesn't really rhyme with much. Appurtenances to the unit are the final building block in our SOC model, and these may be the most difficult to understand. As we mentioned in Chapter 1, an *appurtenance* refers to any common element (or right) where the exclusive use of that element (or exercise of that right) "goes with" the unit and can rarely be separated. This is the part that gets people: You own the right to use the element exclusively, but you can never sell that right independently of the unit. This is slightly different from a regular limited common element, but only in that the association generally has far more control over (and responsibility for) appurtenances.

The classic example of an appurtenance is a unit owner's membership in the governing association—that membership can never be transferred except with the unit itself. Voting rights are also a standard appurtenance. But other good examples, in a condominium anyway, might be your parking space or storage locker; in an HOA, you would generally own your driveway, and in a co-op, you wouldn't really own much of anything. The developer may have divvied up all the parking spaces and assigned them to individual units, and then (in the original documents) expressly designated the spaces as permanent appurtenances. They are attached to the unit forever. The "forever" part is the most important, because it presents courts with both a right and a duty to reunite those elements if they are ever separated.

Take the following example, borrowed (with the addition of a little artistic license) from dozens upon dozens of court cases and arbitration rulings around the country. Unit 406 at the Los Mira Lane Condominium has been assigned a beautiful parking space, one of the few under cover and shielded from storm winds. Unit 107, a much smaller unit, was assigned a space along the highway, near an overpass frequented by hookers, junkies, and personal injury attorneys. The owners of Unit 107 offer to pay the owners of Unit 406 an obscene amount of money to swap parking spaces, and these two owners seal the deal. Money and parking spaces change hands, and as far as anyone in the condominium knows, Unit 107 is now the unit with the prime appurtenant parking space.

Twenty years pass. Unit 406 is eventually sold to a young family with two children. These owners aren't particularly fond of being parked next to a shantytown, so they do some digging. After reviewing the original records of the building, they discover that they have the wrong parking space. They then sue the association to have the space returned to their unit.

In court, the owners of Unit 107 protest that they paid good money for their parking space, which they've been using for years without complaint. These new owners can't possibly rip it out from under them! But according to the judge, they can do just that—and she's absolutely right. The moral of the story: Even if one unit "sells" an appurtenance to another unit, and even if money changes hands, and in fact even if all parties act as if a legal transaction has occurred, the appurtenance can and must revert to its original unit when that unit demands.

It's worth noting that there is a potential exception to this rule: Occasionally, an SOC's documents will expressly allow a unit owner to transfer a certain appurtenance. In addition, some jurisdictions now recognize the right of unit owners to exchange appurtenances permanently with association approval, but the law is still rather unsettled on this issue.

So if you're about to buy a condominium and the owners show you your beautiful parking space, near a brook and a nesting family of robins, it would behoove you to make absolutely certain that it is in fact your parking space. Because if it is not, and down the road someone rightfully complains that the space is hers, you're going to lose it. Check the original documents to see if they allow the transfer of appurtenances, and demand that the management office look up the assignment of appurtenances in the original records. Only then can you be certain of what you're buying.

Another note of interest: Appurtenances must travel with the unit, even if the original owner still owns a unit within the building. Consider the example of a resident who owns two units in Los Mira Lane, along with two appurtenant parking spaces. One space is clearly superior to the other. When the resident sells one of his units, he attempts to keep the good space for himself, even though it's actually assigned to the unit that he's selling. This kind of machination is often illegal, and it can be undone by the courts at any time. On the whole, appurtenances are permanent attachments; they can never be broken.

What, then, are some other appurtenances that you may own? Two examples would be your inalienable rights to access your unit and to use the common elements and other association property. But the most important thing to remember is this: If the right or element is appurtenant to the unit, it belongs to that unit forever, no matter what. *Appurtenance* may not rhyme with much, but it's a very powerful word.

UNIT OWNER RESPONSIBILITIES

So now you know what you own, both by yourself and together with a few hundred acquaintances. But this ownership doesn't come free. What exactly are your *duties* to the association and to your co-owners? Clearly, the principal responsibility of any unit owner is to help pay, through assessments, the cost of property maintenance. While this issue will be discussed in detail in Chapter 9, here are some of the basics.

Every month (or quarterly in some communities) you will receive a bill for your portion of the common expenses. This bill will be divided either equally or by unit size, depending on your SOC documents. It is your number one responsibility to pay that bill! If owners don't pay, the association cannot maintain the common elements. In most states, the penalty for nonpayment of maintenance will be extreme; the association will have the power to put a lien on your unit (basically a legal notice that there is money due, and that they have first dibs should you default). If you still do not pay after a specific period of time, the association may foreclose on the unit (that is, sell it out from under you in order to pay your debts). So when you buy a unit in a condominium, you have to remember that maintenance assessments are constant, variable, and inviolable. This is not rent; this is a common collection of money used to pay the collective operating costs of your home. You can't choose not to pay because you aren't happy with the building, the board of directors, or the services the association provides. If you don't pay, you lose your home.

Depending on the state, you may also be required to pay money toward a *statutory reserve*. The State of Florida, for example, mandates that all associations prepare a budget that includes a set-aside of funds to cover future maintenance, such as the spalling of concrete or roof repairs. This reserve can be very significant—in a new luxury condo, perhaps in the midsix figures per year. Again, this amount is split between all the owners and will be included in your maintenance.

In addition to a statutory reserve, associations may also choose to collect a *voluntary reserve*. Again, this is money put aside against future repairs or restoration projects—essentially, a long-term savings account designated for large projects or emergencies. A voluntary reserve can be collected as a line item in the budget, with the money usually put into some form of interest-bearing savings program (such as a CD or a mutual fund).

Occasionally, though, you can expect also to be responsible for a *special assessment*. A special assessment is used to pay for one-time expenses or specific repairs that are not budgeted. For example, let's assume an anonymous, drunken, 400-pound spring breaker does a cannonball in the pool and destroys the Diamond Brite, necessitating a $20,000 repair. It's doubtful that the association budgeted for such a contingency, so unless there is a significant reserve, it'll have to specially assess owners to collect the cash. As with your regular assessments, failure to pay can result in a lien and a foreclosure. Special assessments are a fact of life in SOCs, so don't be surprised when they arise. Some associations will have an "emergency" or "contingency" line item in the budget for just such occasions, but even that doesn't cover every variable.

In addition to paying your share of the maintenance, as a unit owner you also have the responsibility to abide by the covenants, rules, and regulations laid out in the documents, and to avoid using your unit in a manner that disturbs other unit owners and denies them the quiet use of their property. Again, the penalties vary for ignoring these rules, but they may include both fines levied and lawsuits brought by the association. We talk in detail about rules and regulations in Chapter 10.

UNIT OWNER RIGHTS

In exchange for abiding by your basic responsibilities (paying your bills and following the rules), every unit owner is provided with an extensive laundry list of rights. The American Association of Retired Persons (AARP) has fiercely promoted its own Bill of Rights for SOC homeowners and has lobbied to get these "rights" passed as laws in most states; in fact, many have been adopted already, while the rest are being considered for inclusion in future laws. We therefore present these rules here, along with our comments.

I. *The Right to Security Against Foreclosure: An association shall not foreclose against a homeowner except for significant unpaid assessments, and any such foreclosure shall require judicial review to ensure fairness.* As a whole, this one sounds great. Why wouldn't we want to protect people from losing their homes? However, let us point out the flip side of this issue: If you are a homeowner who pays your bills, you're going to be the person financially carrying all of your neighbors whose unpaid assessments are below the threshold. So this protects the homes of those who can't (or won't) pay, but punishes everyone else. Not our favorite policy.

II. *The Right to Resolve Disputes without Litigation: Homeowners and associations will have available alternative dispute resolution (ADR), although both parties preserve the right to litigate.* No complaints here—less litigation is always a good thing.

III. *The Right to Fairness in Litigation: Where there is litigation between an association and a homeowner, and the homeowner prevails, the association shall pay attorney fees to a reasonable level.* Again, this presents no real problem, but remember who the association is—you. That means when your neighbor sues your condo and wins, you pay his bill.

IV. *The Right to Be Told of All Rules and Charges: Homeowners shall be told—before buying—of the association's broad powers, and the association may not exercise any power not clearly disclosed to the homeowner if the power unreasonably interferes with homeownership.* Laws in every state provide that a person is on *constructive notice* (meaning that he or she is legally presumed to have knowledge of something, whether or not that is the case) of anything in the public record, which includes association documents. Whether or not this rule is a problem depends on how it is applied. Does it mean the manager has to read the documents out loud to every new owner, or does it mean he or she can hand new owners a boilerplate disclaimer?

V. *The Right to Stability in Rules and Charges: Homeowners shall have rights to vote to create, amend, or terminate deed restrictions and other important documents. Where an association's directors have power to change operating rules, the homeowners shall have notice and an opportunity, by majority vote, to override new rules and charges.* The first part isn't a problem, but look at that bit snuck in at the end about the homeowners' right to override new charges. This is going to come up later in the book (Chapter 9), but the basic point can be made here: The owners of an association have wildly varying interests, not all of which take into consideration their neighbors. To avoid a minority rule, elected representatives should make the financial decisions.

Imagine a Southern resort condominium. It's common for more than half the residents to be part-timers, sometimes using the property as seldom as one week per year. Now, assume that the building is falling into disrepair, and the board, consistent with its duty to maintain the common elements, passes a special assessment to clean up the property. The part-timers, however, don't care if the property remains spotless year-round. They only care that they have a pool for the week they come to visit, and that they have as few expenses as possible. Under the AARP's policy, these part-timers could vote against the assessment, and the building's property value would plummet, destroying the investment of the other owners. Sound far-fetched? Well, it happens all the time. If you're not worried about this particular rule, you will be by the time you've finished this book.

VI. *The Right to Individual Autonomy: Homeowners shall not surrender any essential rights of individual autonomy because they live in a common-interest community. Homeowners shall have the right to peaceful advocacy during elections and other votes as well as use of common areas.* This one's fine with us.

VII. *The Right to Oversight of Associations and Directors: Homeowners shall have access to records and meetings, as well as specified abilities to call special meetings, to obtain oversight of elections and other votes, and to recall directors.* A big *yes* on this one, and in fact this is the law in almost every state already.

VIII. The Right to Vote and Run for Office: Homeowners shall have well-defined voting rights, including secret ballots, and no directors shall have a conflict of interest. A very reasonable policy.

IX. The Right to Reasonable Associations and Directors: Associations, their directors, and other agents shall act reasonably in exercising their power over homeowners. Again, this is more or less the law throughout the nation.

X. The Right to an Ombudsperson for Homeowners: Homeowners shall have fair interpretation of their rights through the state Office of Ombudsperson for Homeowners. The ombudsperson will enable state enforcement where needed, and increases available information for all concerned. This covenant aims to level the field for dispute resolution—another great idea that protects homeowners.

So what did we learn from Chapter 3? Every SOC is built from certain standard building blocks—starting with the unit and continuing through the common elements that you own jointly with all of your neighbors. In exchange for this ownership interest, you have a responsibility to pay for the upkeep of the common property and to abide by the rules set forth in the documents. Essentially, everything you need to know about your SOC you learned in kindergarten: You get what you get, and you don't get upset. Next up: the governing documents—the second most important bible that you'll ever own.

WRITTEN IN STONE?
(THE GOVERNING DOCUMENTS)

If you were to ask the question "Why do community associations exist?" you would get two basic answers: first, to more efficiently maintain an SOC through shared financial responsibilities, and second, to enforce a set of rules and operational guidelines that governs conduct while helping to maintain your property value. That's it in a nutshell! Shared maintenance and rules—that's why we're here.

We discuss maintenance in detail when we talk about the role of the association (in the next chapter), but for now we'd like to devote some time to talking about rules. Unquestionably, the most common problem faced by prospective SOC buyers is understanding that there is a set of rules that will legally govern conduct in and around their new home. This is one of the most distasteful issues that will arise in any shared ownership community. And most of the ire is directed at the directors and the weapon they wield against the owners in an attempt to maintain community chivalry, unity, and honor—their Excalibur: the governing documents.

As we explained in Chapter 1, SOCs are legal constructs; they would not exist if not for the laws of various states. More specifically, they are an odd combination of two dissimilar (and often conflicting) areas of law: property law and contract law. The property law side governs such issues as liens, mortgages, and rights of alienation. The contract law side governs the documents.

Your documents are a permanent, legally binding contract between yourself, your community, and your co-owners—which is why they are sometimes called *contractual constitutions*. These rules of operation pass from generation to generation, perpetually, until the community is terminated. You've heard the saying "Ignorance is not a defense"? It applies quite nicely to your documents. When you buy a unit in an SOC, whether from the developer or from a unit owner, you are acknowledging that you are aware of and have reviewed the governing documents of the community, which are part of the public record. You can't say you didn't know they were there. You can't argue that you forgot to read them. You can't claim that you didn't understand them. You can't say that you weren't certain they applied. You can't even point out that they were never provided to you. By law, every owner is on constructive notice of matters in the public record—and that includes your documents, whether you've read them or not. The documents, like any contractual covenant, are inviolable, so you need to understand not only the rights they provide but also the responsibilities they command.

PUBLIC LAWS

Before we go into greater detail about what the documents are and why every SOC has them, let's first discuss the set of rules that take precedence over the documents: the laws of our government.

When dealing with the rules of any society, the natural hierarchy must be followed to determine which regulations trump other, more or less restrictive requirements. This process is no different when it comes to SOCs. The first category, preeminent in all situations, is the laws of the United States of America: the Constitution, the Bill of Rights, and subsequent treaties and statutes. Federal law gets first dibs when it comes to applying regulations to your home—although admittedly, federal law arises fairly infrequently in the context of the community association. The most common questions involve issues of free speech (Can a quasi-governmental community association prevent its members from posting signs or holding meetings on common property?); discrimination (Can an association restrict certain protected classes from buying or renting units? Senior retirement communities, we're talking about you!); and disability (What modifications or alterations must be permitted to accommodate handicapped residents?). All of these issues will come up again later, particularly in Chapters 10 and 13. For now, it's mainly important to understand that the federal government establishes the law of the land.

The next tier includes the most commonly applicable set of regulations: state laws. The fundamental existence of SOCs relies on statutes passed by state governments that describe the contractual relationship between owners and their mandatory membership association. Because the United States is a republic, most laws governing day-to-day operations are left to the states to pass and promulgate. You can expect your state's laws and regulations to be both extensive and very applicable to the operation of your SOC.

There are laws that govern safety (fire or police department), construction (building department), and even your pool (health department). Code enforcement, zoning, drainage, community activities, waste management—just like in a private home, every element of your life in an SOC will be regulated by the basic laws, which vary from state to state.

Just below these state laws in importance are the similar laws passed by county or municipal governments; for example, the city might regulate the direction of traffic in your driveway or mandate that dog poop be removed from public areas. It's also probable that your association will have to abide by various local housing discrimination laws, which often prevent communities from discriminating against same-sex couples. (Note that many antiquated documents of older SOCs still contain proscriptions against non-blood-related families living in the same unit!)

While this collection of laws may sound chaotic, some method to the madness has emerged in recent decades. To date, twenty-five states have passed into law some form of either the Uniform Common Interest Ownership Act or its sister law, the Uniform Condominium Act. Written by experts in SOC operations (including one of the authors of this book), this set of laws has been promulgated as a means of universalizing rules and regulations for SOC home ownership. So if you're lucky enough to live in one of these states, you can expect the Uniform Act's judicial opinions and rulings to apply (more or less). The ultimate goal is for every state to adopt some version of the act, thus ensuring that community association practice is standardized throughout the country.

So first, you must look to your government—federal, state, and municipal. These public laws trump anything in your SOC's governing documents (which are essentially a private contract), no matter how many unit owners agree to a regulation. That is, even if 100 percent of current owners wish to pass a rule banning children from the pool, this would be a clear violation of federal fair housing laws (and possibly those of your state, too). Or maybe you want to save money by turning off all the lights in the common areas after midnight—more likely than not, your city fire marshal will have some choice words about this. We're all beholden to "the Man"; what the authorities say, goes.

PRIVATE LAWS

All the rest of the covenants, restrictions, and rules that govern your life in an SOC are private laws—laws created through contracts between private parties and then recognized by the government as binding. Collectively, these laws are referred to as the *documents*. And, like the public laws, the private laws have an order of importance as well.

The top tier of your community documents is usually known as the *declaration*. In a condominium, it will be the appropriately named *Declaration of Condominium*. In an HOA, you'll find a *Declaration of Protective Covenants, Conditions, and Restrictions* (the aforementioned CC&Rs). In a cooperative, there will be corporate *articles and bylaws* as well as a *proprietary lease*.

The declaration is the cornerstone of the master documents filed by the developer, and it contains all the most basic rules that govern the community. In fact, this document is so important that it is generally constructed in a standard, recognizable manner. Following is an outline of what you can expect to see in a typical declaration:

1. *Property Subject to the CC&Rs*. Generally there is a legal description attached as an exhibit to the documents, defining the real estate that underlies the SOC and is subject to the documents.

2. *Introduction and Definitions.* The declaration next specifies the legal definitions for various terms applied in the documents, from general phrases such as *association property* to very specific words such as *cabana*.

3. *Unit Boundaries.* This section of the declaration generally describes, in very exacting detail, the boundaries of all units and common elements; it specifies which property is considered a part of the unit, a limited common element, a common element, a common area, association property, an appurtenance, or an *easement* (the right of a person who doesn't hold property to use someone else's property for a specific purpose).

4. *Governance.* This section encompasses a number of separate areas that may include rights of alienation, how the documents can be amended, voting rights, association responsibilities, unit owner responsibilities, and additions and alterations.

5. *Operations.* The various provisions dealing with operations specify the structure of the board of directors, the powers of the board and the association, and such issues as insurance and casualty.

6. *Determining Assessments.* This section defines the factors that go into promulgating the budget and ascertaining how the costs of operation are to be prorated among the unit owners.

7. *Occupancy and Use Restrictions.* While there is often a separate document outlining specific rules and regulations, this section of the declaration will present very basic and inviolable restrictions, such as occupancy rules, pet restrictions, basic nuisance provisions, leasing rules, and improvement regulations.

8. *Amendments.* Just like the laws of any democracy, the documents are not chiseled in stone; under most circumstances they can be amended to meet the changing needs of the unit

owners. The amendments section describes the process that must be followed to amend the documents, including how approval is obtained.

In addition to these sections, you can expect to find a host of miscellaneous provisions that may specify the process of transition from developer control, clarify mortgagee rights, and contain various "cover your tuchus" regulations included by the developer. In fact, it's not uncommon to find restrictions imposing impossible voting thresholds that must be met before an association may sue a developer; rest assured that in many states such covenants are not enforceable.

The second category you'll find in the hierarchy of your documents is the articles of incorporation. The articles are usually a brief, dry, and boring document that delineates specific elements of the association's corporate structure from its official name to whether it is a for-profit or not-for-profit corporation to the names of the officers at the time of incorporation.

The next level of documents is the bylaws. While the declaration and the articles provide the who, what, where, when, and why of community living, the bylaws provide the how—the specific corporate rules that must be followed by the association in governing the community. The bylaws lay out the various meetings that must be held (such as an annual membership meeting); owner voting requirements; the number of directors and officers, as well as their positions and responsibilities; how to fill vacancies on the board or remove a board member; terms of directors and officers; practices used in taking minutes; various committees to be organized; and all other issues of corporate governance. If you need to know whether your community follows any specific rules of parliamentary procedure (such as Robert's Rules of Order, discussed in Chapter 7), then look to the bylaws.

As you may have guessed, there is often some overlap between the categories covered by these three documents, and the rules aren't always consistent with one another. So what do you do if the articles of incorporation specify that the association must have five board members, but the bylaws state that no more than three directors may serve at any given time? That's where the hierarchy of laws comes into play. If there's a conflict, the top document controls—and in this instance, that's the articles of incorporation. However, there is a confusing wrinkle: The courts have noted that you must endeavor to read the documents as a whole if possible, and to solve conflicts by determining the intent of the drafters (pari materia is the lawyerly Latin term). So if the declaration specifies that there should be no fewer than six board meetings per year, and the bylaws require one meeting per month, then clearly those provisions can be read in concert to require twelve monthly meetings of the board.

Last on the list are the rules and regulations, always the most specific laws that govern community conduct (some of these rules are repeated in the text of the declaration as well). It's here that you may find rules relating to pets, commercial vehicles, use of the common elements, contractors, nuisance, dress codes—all the nitty-gritty details that will affect your day-to-day life. As we explain in Chapter 10, the rules recorded in this public record hold more weight than any rules that may be passed by the board of directors after turnover. Either way, these are the rules that regulate your day-to-day conduct, so you need to become familiar with them. You can't put a 1,000-pound spa on your balcony and then become indignant when the board decides to enforce the existing rule against hot tubs. And even if your ex-wife threatens to send Droopy to the pound, if the rules say no dogs allowed, then it's no dogs allowed.[1] By far the majority of published arbitration decisions involve rules violations, usually by owners who claim either that they didn't realize there was a rule or that the rule isn't fair. Neither is a legitimate defense. Following the rules is part of living in an SOC—rebels need not apply.

So that explains what's included in your documents—your holy bible of community living. How do you get your copy? After all, you can't reasonably expect the Gideons to leave one in your nightstand!

In some states, the developer is required to provide every unit purchaser with an accurate copy of the documents upon closing. In others, it's up to the buyers to make sure that they are aware of the documents, which are part of the public record. Under the Uniform Act, any "dealer" must provide the buyer with a copy of the public offering statement (or prospectus)—but the act is silent on providing the community documents. In any event, you can generally obtain a copy from your management office or board of directors—sometimes you will have to pay a fee to cover the cost of printing. As a last resort, if your association is especially recalcitrant, head down to the local office of records—and bring quarters for the copier. One way or another, make sure you have a copy of your documents. Because of constructive notice, you can't argue that you've never seen them, even if you actually never have.

AMENDING THE DOCUMENTS

When the founding fathers of the United States wrote the Constitution, their great wisdom was in understanding that times change;

---

1 The notable exception to this rule comes from the Fair Housing Act, which mandates that service or support animals be allowed on any property. More on that in Chapter 10.

they knew they could not have all the answers to what the future held. Therefore, they provided a means to amend their laws—to update them as dictated by a supermajority of citizens.

In contrast, developers and lawyers tend to believe that they do in fact have all the answers. But perhaps in an unconscious nod to our heritage, they also typically provide for a method to amend SOC documents. There are many different reasons that an association might want to amend one or more provisions of its declaration, articles, or bylaws. As the community grows, it might become necessary to add to the board of directors or to modify the basic operations of the association. Maybe the rate of absenteeism is so high that the association would prefer to set a lower threshold for future amendments or a lower quorum requirement to conduct business. Perhaps the members would like to provide an official means for fining residents and filing grievances in case of rules violations. Because community documents try to address hundreds of potential conflicts, they may vary greatly in volume, quality, and reasonableness. Remember that your building's original documents were written by a developer who never had any intention of living in the community, and he or she may or may not have secured the assistance of an attorney in drafting the provisions. It's quite possible that the starting platform for your association's rules and requirements leaves a lot to be desired.

The process of amending your documents is going to depend upon two factors: the laws of your state and the provisions stated in the documents themselves. States typically provide some minimum threshold that is required to amend declarations or bylaws, or at least provide a percentage to use if none is specified in the documents. Once again the hierarchy of laws comes into play. So if the bylaws say that it takes a majority of owners to amend a rule, but the declaration says that it takes 75 percent, you have to follow the more stringent requirement in the overriding declaration. And if the state statute provides that 80 percent assent is required, then the statute would control the outcome. To abide by the law, start at the top and work your way downward.

Note, however, that each of the various documents may establish its own voting requirements that apply only to amendments of that particular document. For example, the bylaws may say that a 50 percent vote is required to amend the bylaws, while the declaration says that a 75 percent vote is required to amend the declaration; those two provisions do not conflict with one another, so each would apply separately. Is your head spinning yet? Be happy that you're not a lawyer and don't have to deal with these tiny distinctions every single day.

Also, you can almost always assume that a membership vote is required to change the documents, not just a vote by the board of directors. The one exception to this would be rules and regulations that govern common area use, which often can be amended or promulgated by the directors as part of their responsibility for managing the association.

For a working example, consider the provisions of the Uniform Act:

- The declaration may be amended only by vote of at least 67 percent of the owners, or such larger number as may be required by the documents (this number can never be less than 67 percent, unless the units are strictly nonresidential).
- An amendment that restricts the permitted uses of a unit or the number of people who can live in the unit may be passed only by a vote of at least 80 percent of the unit owners (or such greater number as established by the documents—but again, never less).
- No amendment may increase the number of units or change unit boundaries without unanimous consent.

In contrast, consider the relevant provisions from Florida's Condominium Act:

- Amendments must be made by a vote of the unit owners, in a manner provided in the declaration.
- If the declaration is silent as to the percentage of unit owners needed to approve an amendment, then a two-thirds vote is required.
- Certain provisions may not be amended without unanimous consent, including:
  - changing the configuration or size of any unit in any material fashion,
  - materially altering or modifying the appurtenances to the unit, or
  - changing the proportion or percentage of common expenses shared by the unit owners.

This unanimity requirement is important, and it brings up the issue of *vested rights*. Certain rights of unit owners are said to be vested, in that they are mature, preexisting rights that can never be modified without the assent of the owner in question. Take, for example, the proportion of maintenance assessments. Assume that the original condominium documents specify that each unit should pay according to size, with the smallest units paying the lowest assessments. Now, let's say that the new president of a condominium owns the largest unit in the building, and he's tired of paying more money than everyone else. After all, he's only one person, so why should he pay as much as some extended families? Besides, he barely ever uses the pool—in fact, he only uses the condo on the weekends, and only then in the wintertime. So he motivates the rest of the board to propose an amendment to the declaration, specifying that all units should pay an equal share of the maintenance.

When voting day comes, Daddy Warbucks has, by some Herculean effort, convinced 99 percent of the owners to go along with his plan. The only holdout is a spunky ninety-year-old woman with four cats and a full-time nurse. And she says, *No way*. No matter how much he begs and pleads, the president is unable to convince the cat woman to vote for the amendment.

The vote fails. That's all there is to it. The woman has a vested right to keep her share of the maintenance exactly as it is, and no force of nature can tear her from her convictions.

The concept of vested rights is fairly new, with the first court decision having been decided only in 2002. As a result, the law is a little gray on what encompasses a vested right, and whether those rights extend to services as well. Assume, for example, that a developer has promised a twenty-four-hour security guard in the prospectus provided to buyers. A reasonable argument can be made that the association must then provide the guard in perpetuity, unless 100 percent of the owners agree to make a change. At the very least, such a change would be a material alteration of the building, and would require a 75 percent vote to pass. We enter an even grayer area if a building had, of its own volition, been providing a service since inception (for example, a doorman). One could argue that that service has become a vested right of the owners and that to make a change would require a large unit owner vote (again, either 75 percent or 100 percent, depending on the legal theory).

In either case, the rule may sound draconian, but realize that it protects the little guy from being manipulated out of his investment, even by a majority of his neighbors. The important thing to remember here is that certain rights are either granted to owners in the documents or inferred from the documents or from building operations; these particular rights cannot be circumvented by any rule without at least a vote of the unit owners, and in some cases that vote must be unanimous. This is one of those areas where, if you're on the board of directors, you should expect to consult the community's attorney. And if you're not on the board, make sure that whatever action the directors are taking complies with the laws of your state. Unfortunately, this may require that you hire your *own* attorney.

In any event, no amendment of the documents is effective until it is recorded in the public record of the county where the community is located.[2] Also note that amendments cannot be applied retroactively, so even if you get that 75 percent vote to punt pooches from the property, it will not apply to any owners who had a dog before the amendment was recorded. To apply a regulation retroactively would be to impair an existing contractual right, and that's simply not allowed.

So that's the way amendments work. Does it all seem clear? If so, give yourself a pat on the back—it's probably the toughest concept you'll encounter in this book.

In summary, every SOC owner must abide by a series of laws, starting with the laws of the government and ending with the private contract known as the *documents*, which can be amended by a vote of the owners. As a member of an SOC, it is your responsibility to be familiar with these laws. Next we discuss the role of the association—what it is, its job, and why it's necessary.

---

2 This isn't entirely true. In some states certain documents don't need to be filed—for example, HOA bylaws or co-op documents. But the vast majority must be part of the public record.

WE'RE ALL IN THIS TOGETHER
(THE ROLE OF THE ASSOCIATION)

In order to understand the structure of any SOC, it may be help-
ful to think of each parcel of undeveloped land as a miniature New
World. Hundreds of years ago explorers visited North America
when much of it was uninhabited (with some notable exceptions).
What they saw was a blank canvas, just as developers today regard
a hundred-acre plot of prime real estate. The settlers pitched in
to build entire towns, just as developers hire hundreds of workers to build modern neighborhoods. Then the settlers realized that
they needed a structure for their towns—a way to operate public

services, collect taxes, and protect residents. Local governments were the obvious answer.

Similarly, you may think of your association as the smallest level of local government.[1] And just as you are a citizen of the United States, your state, and your city, you are also a citizen of Lake Swaying Cypress Retirement Resort and Condominium—aka, a *member*.

Membership has its privileges. Each unit owner in an SOC is automatically a member of whatever association operates the community, whether he or she wants to be or not (thus the term *mandatory membership association*). This membership right is appurtenant to the unit and can never be severed so long as you remain a unit owner. You have the right to participate in elections, to attend meetings, and generally to have your voice heard—the same rights you have as a citizen in any democracy.

Membership also has requirements. You have the duty to contribute financially to the upkeep of the community (taxes) and to abide by the covenants, conditions, and restrictions imposed by the developer (laws). Basically, when you buy a unit in any SOC governed by a mandatory membership association, you have bought yourself not only a home (in the form of a condo, an HOA, or a co-op) but also an extra level of government. Depending on your idea of citizenship, this can be either a boon or a nightmare.

Every owner is a member of the association; however, this does not mean that owners can be held individually liable for the acts of the association. That is, if the association discriminates against a minority or sexually harasses an employee, that person cannot then sue each unit owner individually for damages—a privilege of membership. However, each unit owner does share in the prorata

---

1 The concept of an association serving as a miniature government brings up an interesting issue: Does the conduct of a private association rise to the level of "state action," therefore requiring that association to abide by the requirements of other public governments (such as allowing unrestricted free speech)? We discuss this in detail when we talk about rules and regulations in Chapter 10.

costs of the association, including both legal defense and any judgments levied against the association—a responsibility of membership. So as strange as it may sound, if you sue the association, even if you win, you will be responsible for your proportionate share of the association's cost of defending against your lawsuit and paying your share of the award (to yourself).

As with public government, the structure of your association can take many different forms. It may be a corporation for profit, a corporation not for profit, an unincorporated association, or a trust. Most states will specify the acceptable types of associations in their statutes (remember, the entire *existence* of these associations relies on statutes). In the vast majority of cases, the association will be a not-for-profit corporation. This raises a very common area of confusion among owners—the difference between a nonprofit corporation and a tax-exempt charitable entity. Tax-exempt entities are charitable organizations or religious institutions that are (as the name implies) exempt from paying taxes. In contrast, a nonprofit is simply a corporation for which the main purpose is not profit, but rather to fulfill the obligations established by its organizer. If a community association has earnings other than contributions from its members, it *is* responsible for paying taxes on that money.

Just as every government has citizens, a community association has members. These members elect a certain number of other "citizens" to serve as their representatives—the board of directors. The board is like Congress—of the people, by the people, and for the people. Then, the board members typically are responsible for making policy and electing officers, who carry out the day-to-day responsibilities of the association and implement the board's policy decisions. More often than not, the officers are chosen from among the directors, but they do not have to be; in fact some documents provide that, other than the president and perhaps the treasurer, officers can come from among the members and, sometimes, even from outside the association.

Before we discuss the specific responsibilities of the association, we should ask ourselves one fundamental question: Why have an association at all? Why add a level of private government to our already busy lives? Why can't owners just make all the decisions for themselves in a broad, representative democracy where every issue is voted upon collectively, in a "town hall" format?

While in a perfect society a town hall-style government might work, in the real world there are a number of issues that prevent any government from operating as a pure democracy, including apathy, inefficiency, and neglect of duty.

First, no matter how civic-minded you are personally, you can assume that more than half of your neighbors either do not want to participate or do not have time to participate in the association government, just as more than half of Americans typically fail to vote. Human nature being what it is, people are characteristically apathetic about government unless life-or-death decisions are being made. For many, it takes more time to consider an average money-saving measure than they would have spent in dollars if they had simply ignored the issue. The entire concept of a democracy is that the will of the majority wins over the will of the minority. But for this to happen, you have to know what the will of the majority is! If in this "pure democracy" only a quarter of unit owners vote on issues, then it's certainly not very representative.

Second, it is extremely inefficient to require a voluminous vote on every issue of operation. Decisions are best made by informed people, yet you can assume that the majority of your neighbors are too preoccupied with their lives (raising children, earning a living, etc.) to make time to inform themselves on association matters. Groupwide votes take time and money to conduct; you need to send out ballots, give proper notice, and present documentation to all voters. By the time a vote is taken on a crucial issue, that issue may have grown worse and the remediation cost may have risen.

Third, the directors and officers of an association have a very specific responsibility to the members, known as *fiduciary duty*. This duty requires all officers and directors to be well-informed, to make reasonable business judgments, and to follow the requirements of the law when making decisions.[2] In contrast, members at large have no duty to be so informed—generally, you will find that most of your neighbors are uninformed about not only the relevant laws but also the basic issues affecting the community.

Here's a good example: The law in most states requires the association to maintain the common elements. It is therefore the fiduciary duty of the board of directors to collect the funds required to keep up the property. Imagine what would happen if the membership voted on every single question of maintenance or expenditure of funds. Certainly, some residents have less interest than others in the upkeep of the common elements. Similarly, short-term investors ("flippers") tend to want to spend as little money as possible on maintenance, thereby maximizing their profit. So if you follow the majority vote, even a five-star condominium will quickly become a worn-out, broken-down shell, because the members are not bound by duty to make decisions that will benefit the entire community. In contrast, it is the directors' and officers' duty to follow the law, which ensures that your property will be kept in a manner that supports the value of your home.

---

2 The "business judgment" aspect of this rule provides that, barring conflict of interest or fraud, board members cannot be held personally liable for decisions that they make in furtherance of their duties. If the board members acted in good faith, their judgment will not be second-guessed by the courts. So you can't sue the board for choosing a lousy contractor—even though it was a mistake, it was a legitimate business decision and the board is therefore protected. If, on the other hand, the board gave the contract to the president's cousin, then all bets are off.

So we've established that the operation of an SOC is best handled by an association of voting members, which in turn is run by a smaller group of elected officials who are responsible for policy making and operations. But what decisions are these voting members required to make? Every association has some basic responsibilities that can be separated loosely into two categories: operations and maintenance.

OPERATIONS

Even the smallest SOC must be run like any other business. The grounds need to be kept by gardeners or groundskeepers; the common areas must be cleaned by housekeeping staff; and upkeep and maintenance tasks must be handled by engineers, construction workers, and painters. In a luxury condominium, there will probably be doormen or front desk staff, and maybe even valet attendants. In five-star buildings, it's not uncommon to find a full-time concierge as well as beach and pool staff (just like a resort).

Of course, someone has to manage all these employees—direct their day-to-day activities, take care of payroll and insurance, pay the bills, and put out the fires. Who gets the job?

The Management Team

As we discuss in Chapter 6, the board of directors of an SOC is predominantly a policy-making body. Its responsibilities include setting guidelines and directing procedure, but not actually managing the affairs of the property.

The officers, on the other hand, do take responsibility for day-to-day operations, and in some of the smallest properties it is these residents who actually manage the building. Of course, this presents a number of problems. First, managing even a small building can be a full-time job, and it is best handled by either a professional manager or a volunteer with a lot of free time on his or her hands. In fact, in many states an officer who, in addition to volunteer duties, engages in management tasks and is compensated for that work would have to be licensed by the state, just like any other professional manager. Second, many condominium officers have never managed a business of any kind, much less a multimillion-dollar property. This style of management, therefore, works only for very small properties with limited staff (maybe a housekeeper and a groundskeeper), and it relies on ready and willing residents with a lot of extra time.

The more likely scenario is that the officers of the association (president, vice president, treasurer, and secretary) loosely oversee the day-to-day operations of the association, as managed by a licensed property manager. This raises an issue that often becomes contentious: Does the association employ a single property manager or a broader property management company? There are pros and cons to each approach.

Sometimes, the board of directors will hire a single competent, trained individual as a property manager, tasked with the responsibility of overseeing the entire operation. This property manager is probably licensed, has been schooled in issues of SOC operations, and is familiar with the specific legal guidelines that the community is required to follow. Essentially, the property manager is the chief operating officer—responsible for oversight of the day-to-day tasks required by the association. The manager hires and oversees employees, directs collections from owners, deals with rules violations, brokers disputes, and coordinates with the association's various professionals (lawyers, accountants, and engineers). If you find the right person, the property manager will ensure that the building runs like clockwork and that the board and officers only have to deal with the big-ticket decisions.

Of course, that's a rather significant *if*. Just like any other employee, not every property manager is brilliant, and some can be downright incompetent. It may take more than one attempt to find a manager who fits the style of your community and meshes with the personalities of the board.

Remember also that a "self-managed" building (i.e., managed by the board, the officers, or a single property manager hired by the association) maintains a number of other employees, all of whom require withholding, payroll, insurance, and workers' compensation. Further, these people are actual employees of the association, so they will be governed by the same discrimination and wrongful termination laws as any other business. The association will also be legally liable for the bad acts of its employees. If one of the housekeepers steals a family heirloom, guess who may be responsible?

Here's a true story from an actual association—and it's merely one of thousands. The concierge of a five-star condominium gets involved in a relationship with a resident. By 8:00 p.m. one weekend, the two of them are seen necking on the couch in the lobby. By 10:30, the concierge is stumbling through the lobby, apparently inebriated. A security guard attempts to take away his keys, but he refuses and leaves the building. At 1:30 a.m. there's a huge crash from the garage. The concierge has crashed his car into a custom Mercedes, smashing the rear end. When the security guard hears the crash, he runs to the scene—and sees the concierge, afraid to face the police, escaping on foot.

In a self-managed association, this actual scenario would have been a nightmare. First, the owner of the Mercedes would certainly sue the association, claiming that the employee damaged his property while on duty. The association, naturally, would have to fire the concierge. Of course, if the concierge were an alcoholic, he might try to file an Americans with Disabilities Act claim, arguing that he is being fired for having a disease (a tenuous argument, given his bad act, but not an uncommon lawsuit). So this single fifteen-minute incident could easily turn into five figures worth of legal bills—and a lot of headaches.

If self-management sounds too risky, consider the other option, which may shield your association from many of the difficulties related to the operation of any corporation: hiring a management company.

A *management company* is a business that specializes in managing SOCs; it may retain a few employees or many thousands. Ordinarily, an association and the management company sign a contract that specifies what services are required and what type of management staff is necessary. The management company then assigns a property manager (either from its own staff or hired through an outside search) to work with the management company to hire the dozens of employees that may be needed. In addition, the management company trains all of its employees, conducts background checks, and secures workers' compensation and insurance. In essence, you are hiring a company tasked with taking a houseful of problems off the board members' plates.

In today's reality, complex and onerous procedures have been developed to ensure that employees are not terminated without an extensive history of bad acts. If you wish to fire an incompetent employee who is a member of a federally protected group, the only way to safely protect yourself from an expensive lawsuit would be to keep the employee on staff while you write him or her up for a series of specific job failures over an extended period of time. Although it's an unfortunate system, this is a reality in today's business world. Using a management company, however, gives the board of directors a tremendous amount of flexibility when it comes to hiring and firing decisions. Don't like the manager? Just ask your management company to replace her—it's as simple as that. You don't care where she goes—she just can't stay here. It's up to the management company to actually fire her or just move her to another property, but that's not your problem. You've paid the management company to provide you with appropriate employees for your property, and most companies will adjust the staff to suit your building's needs—just make sure this privilege is written into your management contract so the company cannot ignore your requests. Because it confers many of the rights but not the responsibilities of making employee decisions, this structure gives the association a lot of leeway.

Of course, there is a price to pay for the benefits that management companies can provide, and in this case the cost is substantial. Management companies don't work for free—their services can amount to a six-figure expense: an annual fee, plus a percentage of every dollar paid out to every employee. There may also be hidden profits, such as relationships between the management company and the various subcontractors brought in to service the SOC; the largest management companies own their own subcontractors, such as landscapers, pool cleaners, and carpet and floor cleaners.

In most associations, you can expect a number of members to object vehemently to the concept of hiring a management company—why pay others to do a job that residents (they believe) can do just as well? They will argue that a second layer of management is simply an extraneous cost.

However, from the perspective of the board of directors, there are a lot of reasons why it might be in the best interests of the association to contract with a management company. A single harassment or discrimination lawsuit could quickly wipe out any savings that the association may have realized by going solo. The management company also helps the association to be more flexible, and provides a continuous flow of approved employees. If you are a board member, unless you truly feel that you have the time to do the job properly, don't be embarrassed to insist that the association consider management services as a necessary expense. It would be well within your reasonable fiduciary duty to do so.

The Legal Team

In addition to finding proper management, an association also is responsible for putting together a competent legal team. The role of the association's lawyers is often confusing to owners and board members alike, as they believe (incorrectly) that these lawyers represent one group or the other.

In fact, the association's lawyer represents the association. He or she will help the board determine how to legally collect assessments, manage board meetings, deal with lawsuits, negotiate with a recalcitrant developer, interpret the association's documents, and enforce the association's rules and regulations. Because SOCs are legal constructs, there are always legal issues that need to be addressed. Find a good lawyer for the association, and have him or her on call at all times, because legal issues will arise every single week and it is the responsibility of the board to obtain professional advice.

However, it is not proper for a board member to ask an association attorney to do work for him or her on a personal level (whether related to the association or not), as this may present a conflict of interest, and it is especially inappropriate for the board member to charge such services to the association. Asking the association attorney to do personal legal work relating to your unit, and then expecting the fees to be paid for, is a clear breach of the board member's fiduciary duty—it's also theft.

Even if the board members were being sued in furtherance of their duties for the association, the association attorney would likely not be able to represent them individually. Because our legal system is designed so that each party's lawyer zealously represents his own client, any appearance of double-dealing is considered a very serious transgression; when a lawyer represents two clients that are adverse to each other, this is known as a *conflict of interest*. The condominium would probably *indemnify* the board members (that is, pay for them to retain their own legal counsel) for their defense against the complaint that they breached their duty to the association; however, as the lawyer already represents the association, he or she cannot also represent individual board members in a private capacity as related to their duties.

It's also important to note that while the attorney represents the association, and thus by extension all of its members, he or she is not precluded from suing an individual unit owner. Courts have stated that a ruling to the contrary would prevent any association from suing its members, and because this would clearly be untenable, the courts have ruled that an attorney can, in fact, represent the association in a lawsuit against an individual member. When would such an issue arise? Very frequently, in fact; collections, lawsuits to recover for damage caused to the common elements, involuntary mental health proceedings, and injunctions are all common examples.

The Insurance Team

Another primary operational requirement for any association is to manage its risk by securing *insurance*, and that means finding a competent and trustworthy insurance agent. This may seem like a moderate obligation, but in some states the insurance load can amount to a quarter or more of the total budget of any community—so it's definitely worth a deeper discussion.

The Uniform Act, as well as the laws of nearly every state, provides that an association must maintain a certain amount of property and liability insurance. As always, the documents for each SOC will specify the minimum level required, whether it be statutory (the Uniform Act specifies no less than 80 percent coverage) or some stricter standard (many properties require the association to maintain 100 percent coverage). If the documents are silent, make sure you check the applicable state law. Either way, even if neither requires that the association carry insurance, doing so would be a prudent business decision.

Property insurance, also called *hazard* or *named-risk insurance*, protects the common elements of an SOC against loss as a result of both natural and manmade perils—fire, water damage, structural failure, and destruction of property by a third party (say, if a train derails and levels the guardhouse). Insurance policies tend to be extremely specific about which hazards are covered and which are excluded. For example, you can expect that terrorist attacks will not be covered. Windstorms (hurricanes) and floods, while clearly examples of hazards, are often excluded from coverage as well; each must be covered by its own insurance program. If you live in a coastal state, your association may be required to secure additional insurance for these hazards. In the United States, almost all flood insurance must be purchased through the National Flood Insurance Program, which offers maximum coverage of $250,000 per unit and no price discounts. An association may be able to find third-party insurance on the open market, but in flood-prone areas this is very difficult.

An association must also purchase *liability insurance*, which protects the corporation (or trust) against lawsuits brought by people who injure themselves on the property. If a resident or guest breaks his or her neck while tripping over that loose tile the association always meant to fix, it is the association's liability insurance which comes into play.

In addition to these basic policies, a prudent association also carries a collection of other optional insurance that can best be recommended by a qualified, quality insurance broker. These may include insurance against employee malfeasance (theft or other criminal acts); director and officer (D&O) liability insurance, which protects board members from the cost of defending against "breach of duty" lawsuits; boiler and machinery coverage (for the repair or replacement of mechanical elements such as elevators, boilers, air conditioners, and generators); and workers' compensation. Insuring community property is not like dealing with household insurance, where consumers typically can choose from several different providers offering different levels of insurance at different costs; often there are only limited options for any type of insurance (and especially in hurricane-prone states), so there isn't much price shopping to be done. Instead, an association should endeavor to find the best service possible from an insurance agent, because ultimately it's the level of service that will determine how well the community recovers from a hazard.

The trend in some states is to give SOCs a new weapon in the war against rising insurance costs by allowing them either to self-insure or to participate in an insurance pool. With traditional self-insurance, the community "insures" itself against future casualties by saving money for the sole purpose of correcting future losses. Of course, to insure against 100 percent of possible losses requires a huge savings account—one that most communities can never afford. However, in an insurance pool, a number of communities contribute money toward a fund that will be used to cover casualties suffered by any one of the participants. While this does limit the initial financial outlay required by each community, such shared insurance pools can prove catastrophic if all the participants suffer a loss at the same time or even in the same year. In that situation, it would not be uncommon for the pool to run out of funds while the communities have no method of replenishing it—short of massive assessments levied against all owners, which to some extent defeats the purpose of insurance in the first place.

So the association is responsible first for operating the property, either by itself or by contracting a management company to do the work. The association must also hire competent legal counsel to advise management and the board on how to work within the legal framework provided by the government and the governing documents. Finally, the association must hire an insurance broker and possibly a number of other professionals, including an accountant and an engineer. Once this operational structure is in place, the association's preeminent duty will be to *maintain* the common elements.

MAINTENANCE

While all state laws provide some version of this rule, the Uniform Common Interest Ownership Act explicitly states that "the association is responsible for maintenance, repair, and replacement of the common elements . . . If damage is inflicted on the common element . . . the association, if it is responsible, is liable for the prompt repair thereof." Beyond the legalese, this just explains that the association has a legal duty to keep up the property and repair it when necessary. The laws in some states are even more explicit, stating that the association has a duty not only to maintain the common elements, but also to collect whatever funds are necessary to do so.

Basically, if your board of directors has one job, one overarching responsibility, it's to make sure that the common elements are properly repaired and kept in as close to original condition as possible. This duty is stated in some fashion in every statute, yet it is often ignored by board members. Why?

Ultimately it comes down to human nature. People want to be liked by their neighbors, and volunteer board members are no exception to this rule. It is emotionally difficult for anyone to make an unpopular decision and consequently to become an instant pariah within the community. And maintenance and repairs cost money— sometimes a lot of money. If you are on the board of your association, the most common refrain you will hear from your neighbors is that their maintenance is too high. Many owners forget to consider maintenance as a constant expense on their personal budgets, and they are totally unprepared for this reality of common interest ownership. Part-time residents in resort-area communities may be especially recalcitrant about contributing any more than the most basic level of maintenance, as the community is not their primary home—simply a permanent hotel room somewhere sunny. It is not important that the walls be freshly painted—only that the pool is open and the air conditioning is working.

Another very common problem occurs due to resident aging. Imagine a condominium called Holly Oaks and Shores, a prime plot of East Coast oceanfront real estate developed in the 1970s. At the time, the community was filled with fifty-something professionals looking for a high-end retirement property. Most were still employed, and they could afford to keep the condominium in the manner to which they had become accustomed—spotlessly maintained and operated.

Fast-forward thirty years. The residents of Holly Oaks, now in their eighties, are living on fixed incomes or Social Security, and they rarely leave their units.[3] They certainly don't care whether the grass has been cut, and they don't want their limited financial resources going toward "frivolities." The board of directors, either made up of or heavily influenced by this majority of members, chooses to allow smaller repair and maintenance items to go uncorrected, lest the expense stimulate the ire of the neighbors. Over

---

3 There's actually a term for this: *naturally occurring retirement community*, or *NORC*. It's also referred to as "aging in place."

time, the property deteriorates from its original splendor into a third-rate retirement home—albeit one built on prime real estate.

A little more time passes. Now the residents of Holly Oaks have begun moving into assisted-living facilities, and they need to sell their properties. To their surprise, they find that their property value is a fraction of their neighbors' in nearby buildings. For one thing, they have never funded a reserve, so buyers know that any repairs will ultimately come out of their own pockets. For another, the building is far from the luxury jewel it once was. So the new owners get their units for a song, and a new community of young professionals and investors begins to move into the property.

This is when the real battle begins. The new residents, looking to improve either their property value or their lifestyle, insist that the board of directors maintain the building to a much higher standard. The board refuses. So the new, younger owners either attempt to take over the board by ousting the current members (who may have been actively sitting on the board for decades) or simply turn every board meeting into a four-hour shouting match. Either way the community is now permanently divided into two owner groups who hate each other—one for demanding funds that don't exist, and the other for allowing this investment to wallow in mediocrity. Welcome to the brave new world of board battles, lobbying, politics, and lawsuits.

Occasionally, a new owner will be successful in revamping the association, and the results can be extremely positive for residents, as in the case of one luxury condominium in Bal Harbour, Florida. The property was built as a premier resort thirty years ago, but because of the aging population, it was allowed to convalesce.

Enter an owner concerned about the deteriorating condition of the property. He managed to work his way onto the board of directors—and ultimately to be elected president of the association. With the assistance of a few like-minded directors, the new president implemented millions of dollars' worth of repairs and upgrades, all paid for by special assessment of the residents. In some cases, he did so without the support of the unit owners. But in a short time, the building was restored to a spectacular level—it is now one of the top properties in the area. The end result? Property values in the condominium have increased substantially, and they are currently among the highest in that market. Owners who opposed the reconstruction can now sell their homes at a substantial profit, reaping far more than the monies they paid out in assessments.

The moral of this story: It is always in the best interests of the board of directors to abide by its legal responsibilities in maintaining the property, whatever the cost to residents and regardless of any objections. Remember the concept of fiduciary duty—the community's residents do not have the same legal responsibilities as the board members, and it is very easy for them to demand that their maintenance not be increased. If you are a board member, however, you have a clear duty under the laws of every state to maintain the property—and it is likewise in the best long-term interests of every community to do so.

Of course, there might be situations where a board reasonably decides that an expense is unreasonable or better left for another time. Often, a board must determine the appropriate level of maintenance in a building, which is largely a judgment call. For example, while it might be nice for an association to have ten full-time painters on staff, it is usually financially impractical. As long as fewer employees can do the job properly, it would be within the board's discretion to hire accordingly or even to outsource the work to competent vendors.

Note that the "reasonableness" issue becomes pertinent here once again. Any board of directors is charged with exercising its duties in a manner that follows ordinary business practices. There will always be some flexibility in determining which expenses must be dealt with immediately and which can wait for a few months until further funds are collected from owners. Always remember, however, that maintenance problems have a tendency to worsen, and it may ultimately cost the association far more to correct a problem down the road than when it first arises. Owners may be miffed about a $1,000 special assessment to shore up the roof—but they will be horrified if, six months later, that roof begins to leak and the repair costs increase tenfold. And whom do you think they'll blame first? That's right—the same directors whom they approached in the first place to demand a delay in the repairs assessment. This is just the way it works. If you're serving on a board, you've been warned.

In addition to the duty to repair the common elements, maintenance extends to services as well. Assume that a building has a heated pool. If the directors were to decide not to heat that pool (to save on expenses), they could arguably be sued for failure to maintain the property. The same argument could be made for a number of services that are provided by associations, such as security and valet. That is, if your building has always provided round-the-clock security until recently, when those security services were cancelled in an effort to cut costs, the association might be legally liable for a theft from your unit.

Naturally, the first maintenance issue to arise involves money: How much is reasonable to collect, and for which repairs? The second most common issue relates to power and authority: When does the association have the right (or responsibility) to enter privately owned property to repair or maintain the common elements? What happens if that private property is damaged by the repair? At the outset, the answer follows basic principle: An association has only such authority as is expressly granted to it by law or through its documents. That said, almost every law in the country gives the association unfettered access to private property for the purpose of maintaining or preventing damage to the common elements. Following is the relevant language from the Uniform Act:

> [T]he association is responsible for maintenance, repair, and replacement of the common elements, and each unit owner is responsible for maintenance, repair, and replacement of his unit. Each unit owner shall afford to the association and the other unit owners, and to their agents or employees, access through his unit reasonably necessary for those purposes.

In many states, this rule is even more strongly worded. Here is a passage from an actual condominium declaration in South Florida that mirrors the language in Florida's statute. It grants the association

> [t]he irrevocable right to have access to each Unit from time to time during reasonable hours when necessary for the maintenance, repair, or replacement of any Common Elements or of any portion of a Unit to be maintained by the Association pursuant to this Declaration, or at any time as necessary to prevent damage to the Common Elements or to a Unit or Units, or at any time to enforce the covenants and restrictions on the Condominium Property.

Clear enough for you? Basically, you can assume that the association has the right to enter your home whenever it's required to do so in furtherance of its duties.[4]

In fact, the association may even have a right to demand that you provide it with a key for just such situations. This is problematic

---

4 Of course, this issue comes up less often in the HOA setting, but you can still foresee situations when an association would at least have to cross over your property, if not actually enter your home—power, cable, telephone, drainage, and landscaping issues all come to mind.

to many residents, who assume that they have the ultimate say over who can enter their home. In an SOC environment, that's just not the case. Arguably, an association could enter your home at any time, even if you have not granted access. In situations involving fire or flood, certainly, it is essential for the association to do so. Even if you manage to refuse access, the association can get a court order to allow its employees to enter your unit—and you will be liable for any damage caused by your recalcitrance. So your best bet is always to cooperate with management and allow whatever access is necessary to complete the job.

You'll be happy this policy is in place when your upstairs neighbor's toilet overflows and this right of access prevents your living room from being destroyed. Now, that doesn't mean that the president should tie up his jackboots and kick down a unit owner's door. A reasonable association would first notify the unit owner (at least to the extent possible, depending on the severity of the emergency) and attempt to get permission to enter the unit. When permission is granted, at least two association representatives should always be present to prevent accusations of theft or damage to personal property. If the unit owner refuses entry, the association representatives do have the right to simply enter, even if they have to break down the door—but if circumstances allow (that is, if there's no immediate risk to the building or other units), the association should instead try to secure a court order mandating that the owner must allow access. One way or the other, though, you can be sure that they're getting in.

You can probably imagine a few obvious examples when an association might need to enter your unit—emergency situations like fire or flood, and nonemergency situations that affect the "quiet use" of other units, such as searching for unusual noises and smells. In fact, these simple nuisance complaints often uncover a common and pervasive problem in a number of communities: compulsive hoarders. There are people, especially older people who may have lost their intellectual faculties, who do not throw away *anything*. That includes trash, food, animal feces, newspapers, books and magazines, and old furniture and clothing. Sometimes, these people are simply suffering from dementia; perhaps they have been "dumped" by their families with the excuse that they are better off living on their own in a luxury condominium than in an assisted-living facility. But other times these people are compulsive hoarders, psychologically unable to throw away garbage (and perhaps suffering from obsessive compulsive disorder).

Either way, this creates a very significant issue for associations. First is the obvious smell problem related to rotting garbage and animal waste. Second is the hazard created by rodents and other pests who live in the mountains of garbage. But these residents, especially those who recognize their problem, are among the most recalcitrant when it comes to allowing association access (mostly due to embarrassment, but sometimes as a result of the actual neurosis). If the association is unwilling to exercise its power to enter the unit, it will almost always have to involve the legal system and obtain a court order. This is a judgment call that is best discussed with the association attorney.

When an association must enter a unit to conduct a repair, there may be concerns about damage caused to the unit by the repair itself. Assume you are living in a condominium and there's a leak below you. Usually, the only way to repair such a problem would be to cut a hole in *your* wall to find the leak. But who fixes the hole—not to mention your $100-per-yard silk wallpaper?

Again, the law has foreseen this issue, but this time the guidance varies dramatically across the country. However, we can draw some generalities.

First (as always), you should look to your documents. Many documents contain an "incidental damage" provision that specifically requires the association to pay for repairs of damage to a unit caused by an earlier repair of a common element. Even without such a provision, if the association has to damage an owned element to access a common element, the result would probably be the same. The association is responsible for the cost of this incidental repair, regardless of reasonableness.

The resolution changes, however, if we are talking about an *improvement* to any form of common element (whether limited or actual). At the moment, case law around the country is split on this issue, but in our opinion the most likely eventual outcome is as follows: If a unit owner makes an improvement to a common element, even if that improvement is approved by the association, it will be that unit owner's responsibility to remove the improvement, allow access for the repair, and then restore the improvement at his or her own cost.

Imagine a high-rise condominium built on an angle, where one owner's balcony is also another owner's roof. Balconies, as established in Chapter 3, are usually limited common elements. So if the association needs to repair your neighbor's roof, it won't matter how much money you've spent on custom marble floors with each 36-inch tile hand matched by Tibetan monks—it will be your responsibility to remove the flooring, allow the repair, and then restore the floor after the work is done. A similar situation arises when hurricane shutters are added to window frames, often a common element. If the association added them as a common expense and now needs to access the windows to make repairs, it must remove and restore the shutters. If, however, you added the hurricane shutters to your unit's windows, it will be your responsibility to have the shutters removed and then to reinstall them once the repair is complete.

Of course, to a lot of people this seems outrageous. Where's the autonomy of home ownership? Where's the fairness? Where's common sense?

However, look at it another way: Should you be held financially responsible for every improvement made by your neighbors? Because, that's exactly what would happen if this rule did not exist. The association would be on the hook for hundreds of thousands of dollars in finishing repairs every time a major building-wide project was pursued, and you would end up paying for the stylistic whims of other residents. Instead, residents will be responsible for their own choices. So before you install custom granite floors on your balcony, make sure that you can afford to replace them in case of the inevitable.

Now, if you've been paying close attention, a third question may have arisen: How do you know which elements the association is responsible for repairing? Actually, this question has two answers, and we will address them separately.

First, the association is responsible for the repair and maintenance of the common elements (though some documents specifically charge the unit owner with maintaining limited common elements such as balconies, windows, and glass). The exact nature of the common elements is described in your documents, but generally it includes anything that is not part of an individual unit. In condominiums, the unit is typically designated as the space inward from and including the surfaces of the four walls. Everything inside the walls is a common element (though sometimes a pipe or wire that serves only a single unit is defined as an owned element). The roof, the balconies, and all common rooms and areas (e.g., pool, clubhouse, gym, spa) are common elements as well. By law, the association is responsible for repairing these elements, maintaining them, and preventing future damage.

Note also what this repair duty typically will not cover—such as kitchen cabinets (even if they were installed by the developer) and lighting and plumbing fixtures. That is, if your toilet breaks, don't call the association. You own it—it's your toilet. Fix the thing. If it flows over and damages the unit below you, and if you were negligent in not fixing it, you'll be responsible for that damage as well as your own. If the association is forced to enter your unit in an attempt to protect the common elements (or another unit) from damage, it might charge you for the cost of the repair as well.[5]

The second response, however, creates a huge wrinkle in this principle, and one that is, frankly, very difficult to understand. Here goes: Even though the association does not have a legal responsibility to repair or maintain owned elements, it *may* have a legal responsibility to carry the risk for repairing those owned elements in the event of a casualty. For example, one state statute requires that, in addition to maintaining the common elements, an association has a duty to provide primary hazard coverage for "the condominium property located inside the units as such property was initially installed, or replacements thereof of like kind and quality and in accordance with the original plans and specifications . . ." What this means is that the association must insure not only the common elements (e.g., the lobby and the building's exterior) but also certain owned elements, such as interior drywall, concrete, doors, or plumbing fixtures—items for which the association is not ordinarily responsible. This particular state law excludes some of the big-ticket owned elements (such as cabinets and flooring), but every law is different, so you should check your statutes.

The distinction, while esoteric, is important. If your toilet breaks, you have to replace it. If your toilet is destroyed in a hurricane, the

---

5 Incidentally, when the association needs to make a repair that displaces you from your unit, it must then compensate you for the cost of alternative housing (i.e., a hotel) while you are out of your home.

association has to replace it—not because it has a responsibility to maintain your toilet, but because it has a responsibility to insure against the loss of your toilet. See the difference? It's very subtle but it does exist, and though it may seem like much ado about nothing, it's important to understand. The association has a duty to maintain certain common elements and limited common elements. It may have an additional duty to insure a greater percentage of the building against hazards, and this often includes a number of owned elements. So if your unit is damaged by a hazard of any kind, make sure you research exactly what the association is responsible for repairing, and under what circumstances.

Maintenance or Material Alteration?

As we've discussed, an association has a duty to maintain the common property, and the result is generally obvious: basic, everyday maintenance. If there's a stain on the wall, you paint over it. If there's a leak in the ceiling, you fix the leak and patch the ceiling. If the elevator breaks, you get it repaired.

What happens down the road, however, when a building element needs to be totally replaced and the association wants to take that opportunity to upgrade? Say, for example, that a condo built in 1970 is painted in then-popular shades of mauve and teal. The entire building needs a fresh paint job, so the board wants to update the color to a more neutral off-white. Or perhaps the paved driveway needs to be resurfaced, but the association wants to install solid marble slabs. Does either of these "improvements" fall under the category of basic maintenance, or do they rise to some different standard?

These types of upgrades are more than likely *material alterations*, and as such they open up an entirely different can of worms. To explain how material alterations work, and what you need to know as either an owner or a board member, we'll discuss a case so pervasive and instructive that we'll mention by name: *Sterling Village Condominium, Inc. v. Breitenbach.* If you ever have to impress your condo attorney, this 1971 case is the one to mention.

A number of units in the Sterling Village condo had external balconies that were originally enclosed with screening. Over time, as the screening deteriorated, some of the owners chose to replace that screening with glass jalousies—shutters with adjustable horizontal slats for regulating the passage of air and light. Of course, this dramatically changed the exterior appearance of the building. The question presented to the court was whether this modification was so significant that it constituted a material alteration requiring a vote of the membership to implement.

The court, in a powerfully compact decision, held that making a material alteration or addition "means to palpably or perceptively vary or change the form, shape, elements or specification of a building from its original design or plan, or existing condition, in such a manner as to appreciably affect or influence its function, use or appearance." The judge then went on to hold that replacing wire screening with glass jealousies is clearly a material alteration, and therefore a vote of the unit owners was required.

How does this affect your community? First, this ruling has been codified into law in many states. While the basic Uniform Act does not address the issue, even if you are in a Uniform Act state you should still check your statute to see if a relevant provision has been added. Most other states will have some version of a "material alteration" prohibition in their laws. Since *Sterling Village*, hundreds of cases and arbitration decisions have dealt with the question of whether a building modification is material (therefore requiring approval of the membership) or immaterial (something the board can change on its own). Among the modifications that have been ruled to be material alterations are changing paint color, changing exterior appearance, changing the use of a common area, adding exterior window guards, or even making wholesale modifications of landscaping.

Returning to the *Sterling Village* scenario, the judicial decision says that the board has to secure a unit-owner vote (the exact percentage will vary by state and according to each community's documents) before repainting the building or upgrading the driveway. This law ensures that a building will never change palpably without the consent of the members.

However, it also makes it extremely difficult to modernize old properties. For this reason, courts have developed a couple of exceptions to *Sterling Village* that help associations cope with large improvement projects. First, under the "maintenance" exemption to the rule, repairs do not need to be identical to the original in order to be permissible; if the change is necessary to aid in maintenance, unit-owner approval may not be necessary. Take the example of an actual condominium involving Chattahoochee—the uncomfortable, pebbly pool deck surface that was so in vogue in the 1970s. When the board needed to tear up the pebbles to repair the corroded drainage system, the directors decided to spend a bit more money and install brick pavers. They theorized that even though the pavers cost a bit more at the outset, this change would reduce the cost of future repairs. The court ruled that this modification was well within the board's powers, as in its reasonable judgment the change was deemed necessary for future maintenance. Since this decision there have been dozens of similar cases, and the key factor in each case was that the deck surface was ready to be replaced and that a different material would be simpler to maintain.

In fact, even a wholesale addition to a property can fall within the "maintenance" exception. The most common example involves the construction of a beach wall or *rock revetment* to protect a coastal building from flood damage and erosion. Adding a new wall to a property is unquestionably a material alteration to the common elements—but when its primary purpose is to protect the property, the courts will allow the addition without unit-owner approval.

Another fallout of this principle is the fact that an SOC's declaration may define in a broader manner which alterations are material, and sometimes may state that only alterations of a certain dollar amount must be brought to a unit-owner vote. But it is unclear how this would play out with a change that is otherwise material. For example, say that a building's declaration states that only expenditures of more than $100,000 must be brought to a vote of the unit owners. The board wants to repaint the building in a new color—bright red—and it will cost only $90,000. Is the color change a material alteration, or is it exempted by the language of the declaration? Only a lawsuit will tell us for certain. Further, there are declarations that give the board a broad power to make *any* material alterations, no matter how significant. Now *that's* a powerful board.

So we've learned that every owner within an SOC is a member of a mandatory association that operates the property. This association has a board of directors, just like a corporation, and probably has hired a manager to actually operate and maintain the common elements. The association may also hire other professionals to help run the business, such as lawyers, accountants, engineers, and insurance agents. Next we discuss the duties and responsibilities of your fearless leaders: the directors and officers. And no, they're probably not stealing from you.

WHO'S IN CHARGE HERE?
(DIRECTORS AND OFFICERS)

A man knocked at the heavenly gate—he was so very old. He
stood where people have to wait for admission to the fold.
"And what have you done," the good Lord
asked, "to gain admission here?"
"I've been a condo director, sir. Each day seemed like a year."
The Pearly Gates swung open wide. An angel rang the bell."Come in
and choose your harp," he said. "You've had your share of Hell!"

When you finished high school, you probably thought that your
days of small-time elections were over—that you'd left behind the

handmade posters, bowls of lollipops, and buttons reading "Vote for Jason." Imagine your surprise to find that the world of junior politics is alive and well . . . in your community association!

It's disconcerting to realize that a majority of grown adults will quite readily involve themselves in a world of little-pond power plays and aggressive ad hominem attacks. Of all the issues involving SOCs, the constitution of the board of directors is probably the most often contested—and perhaps the most personally contentious. Because, at a basic level, there are three types of people who most frequently run for a board position:

- those who have always been in charge and therefore feel entitled to the position;
- those who have never been in charge, and therefore feel that they deserve the position; and
- those who have a genuine interest in helping the community.

Given that you are taking the time to read this book, if you are interested in getting involved in your community government you almost certainly fall into the third category—but we're sure you know plenty of people who belong to the first and second groups as well. Furthermore, it's not uncommon for these lines to blur; a candidate could genuinely want to serve the community, but may also feel that he or she is *entitled* to serve the community. Plus, some candidates may have specific and preeminent goals (such as lowering maintenance or improving security) that, for them, supersede all other business—and might turn them into caricatures of their normally mild-mannered selves. So what happens when you mash together a score of gigantic egos, a dash of personal vendetta, the heartbreak of high school, and a handful of well-meaning members? You get the angst, chaos, and mass hysteria that make up your typical board of directors.

The high school election model is predominantly about popularity. You lobby for better school lunches, a longer recess, and more field trips, and if you achieve even a fraction of what you're promising, you will quickly find that you've become a *macher*, a Big Man on Campus. But if you serve on an HOA, condominium, or co-op board, plan on being hated by at least a few of your neighbors. People may think that running for a directorship is like running for class president, but in fact it's a lot more like running for Congress. The directors are responsible for taxation (assessments), law enforcement (rules and regulations), welfare (collections), defense (security), and social programs. Even the most popular American politicians rarely have an approval rating greater than 70 percent or 80 percent. Let's assume that you're the president of a three-hundred-unit condominium, and that your approval rating is a staggering 90 percent. That still means that thirty of your neighbors think you're an idiot. More typically, at least 30 percent of your neighbors will disapprove of your performance—meaning that nearly one hundred people who live within three hundred yards of you think that you're doing a poor job. Will that make you uncomfortable? Then you'd better think twice before running for the board.

It's a little sad, really, because there are plenty of well-meaning, competent candidates for board positions who simply are not suited to the reality of politics, just as not everyone with good ideas would make a good congressperson. Make no mistake—serving as a director of any organization will involve politics, and SOCs are no exception.

So before you throw your hat in the ring, make sure you're comfortable with the notion that you can't please everyone. You will be forced to make some decisions, as a matter of either law or necessity, that will be quite unpopular. If you're OK ignoring the dirty looks you'll get at the pool, then a directorship may be in your future.

While we've painted a scary picture of association politics, there are certainly numerous exceptions to this rule. There are communities in which a small group of well-meaning, educated, and cogent professionals take the time to be informed on the issues, to advise themselves of their legal duties, and to discuss their decisions openly and with adequate comment from other owners. But the bigger the board gets, and the longer the directors have been in power, the more likely it is that personal issues will supersede the welfare of the community.

Furthermore, boards—like the communities they represent—are microcosms of society. As a whole, officers and directors are not criminals—but there's a chance that some are, just as criminals (not to mention drunks, imbeciles, head cases, and nut-jobs) exist in the world at large.

Does this mean that all hope is lost? Should you throw in the towel and accept that your home is operated by a group of unqualified has-beens and puffed-up shirts? Of course not—you're committed to positive thinking. After all, you're reading this book! By the time you've completed this chapter, you should have a very strong understanding of the responsibilities of your officers and directors, as well as what you can do about those who refuse to follow the rules. If you're brave enough, maybe it will be your turn to hand out the buttons and lollipops.

Let's start the discussion with some basic definitions. As we mentioned in the last chapter, the all-member association that operates your community is run by an elected board of *directors*. Directors are the corporate managers of the association. They meet on a regular basis, either in person or by some electronic means (such as a teleconference). Their job is to make policy decisions that affect the operation of the community—budgeting, expenses, renovation projects, rules and regulations, hiring and firing, choosing various professionals (such as lawyers and engineers), and resolving disputes.

Of course, someone needs to actually implement those policy decisions, and that job falls to the *officers*. The four main officers of any corporation are the president, vice president, secretary, and treasurer; other officers may include a parliamentarian (who is in charge of proper procedure and decorum at board meetings), an assistant treasurer, an assistant secretary, etc. These people are responsible for all the day-to-day duties—monitoring the books and finances, assigning tasks to the employees, taking notes at meetings, dealing with emergencies, and generally making sure that the SOC runs smoothly. The officers are usually chosen by, and are beholden to, the directors. The vast majority of corporate charters specify that the president and the treasurer must also be board members, and in a corporation as small as an SOC it is likely (though not necessary) the officers will all be directors as well.

An officer can be any interested resident, however, and in fact many documents don't even require officers to *be* residents—only unit owners. It's a job. Depending on your documents, your association could actually hire someone to serve as an officer, just as a corporation might hire a raider to come in, gut operations, and leave a business that is less costly to operate. Your community's articles of incorporation or bylaws should tell you who can serve on a board, how officers are elected, and whether officers or directors need to be owners. At the very least, directors typically are required to be a title owner of record for their unit.

While board members are policy-making volunteers, officers may be paid in some cases, even if they are also directors or owners. Officers and directors may, of course, be compensated for work that is *unrelated* to their board service, such as when the president of an association is also the acting manager (as sometimes happens in very small developments). Officers and directors also can be reimbursed for appropriate expenses that are required to conduct their jobs—up to a point. It comes down to common sense: Photocopying, phone bills, and office supplies would be appropriate expenses, while paying for an actual photocopier or a telephone would be a bit more questionable.

Also, an officer or director may need to hire an attorney, but this doesn't necessarily mean that the association picks up the bill. As a general rule, if the defense is related to that person's duties, the association will pay for the lawyer—but it gets a bit tricky when association members begin to fight among themselves. For example, in one case a number of board members hired an attorney to defend them against an attempted recall (basically, the other owners were trying to kick them out of office). Even though they argued that the attorney was retained to ensure a "fair" election, the court ruled that the directors could not be reimbursed for the expense, as it related to the officers as individuals and not to their service to the association.

The required qualifications to serve as a director or an officer also vary depending on the state statutes and the association's documents. In Florida, for example, convicted felons are not allowed to serve as directors (until five years after their civil rights have been restored), nor may anyone serve who is delinquent in assessments. Many other variables may determine eligibility. Ultimately the documents are a private contract, so wide latitude is given when it comes to the provisions.

So the association has officers and directors. The directors set policy, and the officers carry it out. But what policy do they set? What exactly do their jobs entail? Loosely, the officers and directors of an association are required to make decisions in furtherance of the association's responsibilities—to maintain the common elements, to collect funds required to maintain the common elements, and to enforce the covenants, rules, and regulations—all because of a legal concept known as *fiduciary duty*.

FIDUCIARY DUTY AND BUSINESS JUDGMENT

We touched on this concept in Chapter 5: In a nutshell, officers and directors have a specific, legal duty to carry out the business of the association—and they can be held personally liable for not doing so.[1]

According to *Black's Law Dictionary* (which is *the* guide to legalese), a *fiduciary* is "a person having duty, created by his undertaking, to act primarily for another's benefit in matters connected with such undertaking." Basically, officers and directors of an association, just like corporate officers or trustees, have a duty to act in good faith—exhibiting trust, confidence, and candor—in the best interests of the other members. Now, that doesn't mean the president should be babysitting or doing your laundry. What it *does* mean is that board members must endeavor to protect the rights and interests of their neighbors, and to protect them from foreseeable risks and liabilities. What it *does not* mean is that the officers and directors must bow to the whims of individual owners, or that they may ignore the duties of the association, even if doing so is in the majority interests of the other members. Instead, the officers and directors have a responsibility to carry out their directorial duties in a manner consistent with the directives of the law, and in a fashion that protects the common property. Edmund Burke, an Irish politician and theorist, put it best: "Your representative owes you not his industry only, but his judgment; and he betrays, instead of serving you, if he sacrifices it to your opinion." This means that responsible board members should do what they think is best for

---

1 When a developer serves as an officer or director of an SOC, as is common before turnover, that person owes the same fiduciary duty to the owners as would any other officer or director. So if the director, serving in an official capacity, acts in bad faith (say, fails to collect maintenance for developer-held units), he or she can be held *personally* liable for any damages. That's why smart developers put their underlings on the board instead of themselves.

the community, rather than cater to the requests of individual unit owners.

That said, it's clear that abiding by this fiduciary duty involves a good dose of personal judgment—and again, there's a rule for just such a situation. It's called the *business judgment rule*. Generally, a director must exercise good faith in making the same decisions that an ordinary, prudent person would exercise under similar circumstances, and in a manner he or she reasonably believes to be in the best interests of the association. The exact rule might be stated differently depending on state statute. The Uniform Act is frustratingly vague, stating simply that "[o]fficers and members of the executive board . . . shall exercise the degree of care and loyalty required of an officer or director of a corporation," but that's better than a lot of states, where the statutes defer entirely to the rulings of case law. Still, you can assume that the officers and directors of your association not only have a fiduciary duty to the members but also must use appropriate business judgment in making their decisions.

The business judgment rule isn't just an obligation—it's also the best legal protection an officer or director will ever have. In any association, every single decision made by a director or officer will be scrutinized by the membership. And there are always litigious people who will sue, early and often, over anything they feel is contrary to their own needs. You assess them? They'll sue. Close the pool for a week? Sue. Paint the stairs? It's the wrong color—sue. Remember that your SOC is a microcosm of society, and think about all the lawsuit-happy people you read about in the papers. There's a good chance one of them is your neighbor! But the business judgment rule, in addition to saying that a director or officer must exercise good faith and make reasonable decisions, also says that those who follow this rule cannot be held personally liable for their decisions. Short of bad faith, fraud, conflict of interest, or gross negligence (lawyers call this *malfeasance* and *misfeasance*), an officer or director of an SOC cannot be successfully sued.

Assume that a naturist condominium, Breezy Acres, is soliciting bids to install a fifty-person hot tub. The board gets proposals from three contractors, compares the prices, checks references, discusses the issue in one or more open board meetings, and gives a $20,000 deposit to the top choice—who promptly runs away with the money. (Of course, no one can chase after him because, well, they're not properly dressed.) So the board members get sued (which, parenthetically, is why a board member should always insist on having D&O insurance). The plaintiff complains that they made a stupid decision and lost his money—and that now they should pay. But the court doesn't care about the end result; all the judge wants to know is whether the directors made the decision in good faith, using ordinary, reasonable judgment. If they did, they will not be held personally liable. The business judgment rule is the toughest shield an officer or director could have.

But let's say that the president of Breezy Acres, Richard Swingsalot, failed to reveal to the board that the chosen contractor was his best friend, and that he coached him on the proper bid amount. That, friends, is *not* good faith. That is a conflict of interest, and it's always a no-no. Richard's going to lose the lawsuit, and he is going to be held personally liable for his bad decision (to say nothing of possible criminal penalties).

It's also important to note that the business judgment rule protects only the officers and directors from legal liability—and not the association. If the board needs to tear up someone's floor to fix a drainpipe and then refuses to repair the floor, the association would eventually lose the lawsuit—but the directors would not be personally liable.

ELECTION PROCEDURES

Now it's time to get into the nitty-gritty: How exactly do officers and directors become officers and directors?

As with any government, election procedures can be either extremely simple or vastly complex, depending on the proscriptions of the state and the wording of the association's documents. For example, the Uniform Act says simply that directors must be elected, and that there must be at least three of them; beyond that, you must check your bylaws or articles of incorporation for the specific procedure. In contrast, some statutes provide a painfully detailed procedure to be followed by all associations, such as the one summarized in this actual example:

- Not less than sixty days prior to an election, the association must give notice and invite those who wish to be candidates to inform the association within forty days of the election.
- Not less than fourteen days prior to the election, the association must mail ballots to owners with a separate return envelope (the statute actually specifies the type and size of the envelopes required!).
- At least 20 percent of eligible voters must send in ballots for the election to be legal.
- Proxies are verboten.
- Ballots may not be removed from the return envelope until the meeting, when this must be done in the presence of unit owners.
- In the case of a tie, a runoff election is held.

These seemingly draconian rules were developed in response to decades of lawsuits involving the fairness of elections, after millions of dollars in legal fees had been spent by associations. So while the rules may seem oddly specific, this makes it difficult to violate them without it being noticed, which tends to keep things fair. If you are in a state that provides very little election guidance, it would behoove your association to take a close look at its bylaws and to make certain that your election procedure is explicit and difficult to challenge. While it may cost more to run your elections, in the long run it could save thousands of dollars in legal fees.

So the association members elect the directors, who then elect the officers—sometimes from among the other directors and sometimes not. It's a system more similar to corporations than to the U.S. government—but it works out rather well. The officers are always beholden to the elected board, and they can be removed at any time if they are not implementing the board's policies.

But what happens when the *directors* aren't doing their job? Who oversees *them*? This comes down to what might be the most misunderstood and underutilized principle in all of community association law: Ultimately the members run the show. It is a universally accepted principle, whether in common law, state statute, or your documents, that a majority of SOC owners may remove one or all board members at any time, for any reason, and replace it with a new board of their choosing. That's a massive power for any citizenry to wield. There's no analogue in our own federal government and probably none in state governments, either.

Of course, this brings up a number of sticky issues. First, in a lot of associations the membership will be so disinterested in their homes (whether because they are part-timers or because they just can't be bothered) that it becomes impracticable to get more than half of the owners to agree to much of anything. Second, even if the owners were to entirely replace the board, the new board members would *still* be obligated to act within their fiduciary duty and use reasonable business judgment—or be subject to a lawsuit. So if you're angry that your board of directors has assessed you for a skyrocketing electric bill, and you organize a recall to oust the louts, the new directors would continue to have an obligation to assess the owners for the electric bill—part of the reasonable costs of maintaining the community. A recall is not a tool that allows owners to get what they want, no matter the circumstance. It is, instead, the ultimate check and balance against the board. If the directors fail to do their jobs—if they truly aren't living up to their obligations— they can be removed at any time.

Finally, if a board member vacates his office voluntarily before his term is up, most documents (and a number of states' statutes) specify that the board may appoint a successor to serve out the term. This saves associations, especially those with large boards, the considerable expense of an interim vote, as proper elections may cost $1,000 or more to conduct.

So the directors and officers of an SOC are the elected representatives of the unit owners, who serve at their pleasure to operate the association. As representatives, the directors and officers owe the members a special legal duty to take actions that are in the best interests of the association and to use ordinary business judgment in making decisions. In the chapter that follows, we reveal ins and outs of the forum used for making these decisions: the meeting.

7 LET'S GET TOGETHER
(CONDUCTING MEETINGS)

Up until this point, we've talked a lot about how an association runs *generally*—the fact that there is a board, that it meets to discuss issues, that it makes decisions on behalf of the other owners. But we have not yet discussed the *specifics*: how these meetings are run and what your rights are as an owner concerning board meetings as well as meetings of the entire ownership.

Let's visit a condominium during its very first membership meeting. Who is in charge? Who decides which people get to speak and when? If you have four members, you have four opinions, and everyone thinks theirs is the correct one. Without some accepted way to organize discussion, this becomes a shouting match, and no one truly hears what the others have to say. Eventually, one or more attendees tire and quit, and the opposing party wins the argument—not very efficient, effective, or practical.

Luckily, early in the creation of modern government (around the fifth century CE), along came the invention of *parliamentary procedure*—a series of rules and laws that specify how meetings are conducted. And though these laws originated in England, Americans perfected them. In 1876 a man named Henry Martyn Robert published his version of the rules, and today *Robert's Rules of Order* is the gold standard of meeting organization. In the modern association environment, a properly conducted meeting should never be without a strong chairperson, a defined order of business (the *agenda*), and guidelines for discussion (like *Robert's Rules*). The expectation of this basic procedural foundation can help new associations avoid a lot of confusion and frustration.

Now, assuming there were absolutely no rules in place, practically any discussion between two or more board members could technically be considered a "meeting." And it wouldn't have to be in person, either—a telephone call, a letter, or even an e-mail would suffice. So what prevents board members from simply chatting with each other casually, coming to a decision on issues, and implementing them—with no input from other owners?

If you guessed "the laws and the documents," you get a gold star. State statutes typically specify procedures that must be followed by associations or, at the very least, by corporate boards. Further, your community bylaws are almost certain to provide even more specific rules that must be followed before any official decision can take place. And nearly all SOC documents dictate that two very important things must occur before any meeting takes place—the posting of *notice* and the establishment of a *quorum*.

NOTICE

It is a very basic principle of SOC government that the owners of record should have the right to attend board meetings, listen to the issues, and often even discuss them with the board of directors, so that the board can make an informed decision. But how do residents know when the board is going to be discussing important issues? Through notice. According to almost every law and document, a board is required to notify both its directors and the owners themselves within a reasonable time that a meeting is going to take place, giving them an opportunity to attend and sometimes even participate. Your state statute may or may not specify this "reasonable" time period, but your documents almost certainly do. This is really no different from how our local governments operate: When your county commissioners are discussing a new roadway, they generally provide notice of the meeting to residents, informing them of their opportunity to present their opinions in a public forum. Note that community associations are *not* bound by federal and state "sunshine laws" that require every meeting of an agency to be open to public observation; these apply to government bodies only and not, in any fashion, to community associations. Instead, associations must abide by whatever open-meeting regulations appear in the state statutes or in the association documents.

What about emergencies? Most laws and documents allow a board of directors to discuss an emergency issue with less advance notice, as long as the decision is then ratified at the next board meeting. But note that "less notice" does not mean "no notice." Numerous judicial decisions about this exact issue have determined that it is not OK for a board to get together secretly and make decisions, using the explanation that it was an emergency meeting. Notice must be provided as soon as practicable, even if that means it's posted right before the meeting is held. Also, remember that "Damn, we forgot to reimburse Sheila for the teapot!" doesn't count as an emergency. No, an "emergency" means just that—a hazard or urgent issue that, if allowed to continue unabated, would result in serious deterioration of the property or harm to people on the property.

Generally, "posting" notice means placing the notice in a predetermined, open, and conspicuous location that can be seen by all residents. If the residents don't check that location, that's their problem—but then again, you can't stick a notice on the inside of a men's room toilet. Usually there is a community bulletin board that will suffice. Some associations will also e-mail their residents (typically in communities where the median age is well below the century mark), and some communities even have a closed-circuit television system for news, notice, and events. In any case, unit owners should be able to find out easily where and when meetings are held.

This is a good opportunity to bring up another concept—the "workshop" meeting (otherwise known as a *caucus*). Some board members have other, more pressing responsibilities than their community associations, and they want to discuss small issues without wasting time or worrying about what they say in front of the owners. A workshop meeting, therefore, is a private board meeting where issues are discussed, but decisions are not made. And they've become very, very common. In many states, they're also very illegal. As we've said, the general principle is that *every* board meeting must be noticed and open to members, and that practically any communication between board members can be considered a meeting. The stricter states have held that *any* communication between an agreed-upon majority of board members (a *quorum*, which we discuss further in the next section) where *any* issue is discussed is construed to be a board meeting, and it therefore has to be noticed and open to members. What if you're discussing something confidential, such as salaries? Doesn't matter. What if you're just discussing issues that will come up at a meeting later in the week? Still not OK. The thinking behind this is that any discussion among board members could result in one or more members making a decision about the issue, when that decision should rightfully be influenced by the input of owners. It's a rigid but very democratic rule.[1]

In the more liberal states, workshop meetings are encouraged as a way to save time and energy at the actual board meeting. In fact, the most recent proposed revisions to the Uniform Act will allow closed executive sessions to be held during board meetings, to discuss any issue that involves a privacy concern, such as personnel matters or contract bids. Even in strict states, association boards often discuss issues via e-mail and make decisions long before they've come up at a meeting—but the fact that it's common practice doesn't make it kosher. This is a subject that, if you're on a board, you should definitely bring up with your attorney. You do not want to make a decision on a $30,000 pool repair at an improperly noticed meeting, only to expend double that amount defending a lawsuit from the one owner who doesn't want to pay his special assessment.

The amount of advance notice required for a meeting varies depending on the importance of the issue being discussed. Ordinarily, forty-eight hours is the gold standard. But sometimes when issues involve rules and regulations, or when budgets are being discussed, fourteen *days'* notice must be provided. Often, notice for this type of meeting must be hand delivered or mailed to residents, rather than simply posted. This is to ensure that members are especially aware of meetings that are likely to have a significant effect on their use of the property.

---

1 The exception to this rule relates to conversations with the association's attorney. Attorney-client communications are *privileged* (protected from public revelation), and therefore these meetings may be held in private.

In addition to advertising the time and place of the meeting, any proper notice should include an agenda listing what issues will be discussed, so that owners may determine whether they need to attend. If an issue is left off the agenda, then it may not be discussed at the meeting unless it is an emergency. (The rules of parliamentary procedure provide very specific requirements for bringing up emergency business in meetings; it must be raised by a super-majority of directors, and any decision made must be ratified at the next meeting.) Some associations have taken to providing only the most general of agendas, perhaps saying that the board will discuss "any and all business that is proper." This may satisfy the letter of the law, but it certainly violates its spirit. The entire concept of providing a notice and an agenda is to allow owners to prepare their comments.

So we've established that, in almost all jurisdictions, any meeting must be open to owners and properly noticed, with a detailed agenda of issues to be discussed. But what exactly constitutes a "meeting"? That's where the quorum comes in.

QUORUM

In reviewing the basic structure of any representative democracy and the various problems it may face, one of the main concerns is that a representative government actually be . . . well, *representative*. That is, if two members of a nine-member board of directors were to vote on a major project, would you feel comfortable that the decision represented the majority of owners? Of course not. If you've gone to the trouble to elect fiduciaries, you want to ensure that their voices are heard. This principle remains the same from the smallest corporation up to the largest parliamentary body.

A *quorum* is the minimum number of members of a deliberative body that is competent to transact business. Ordinarily, a quorum is equal to half plus one (a simple majority), but it can be any amount specified by statute or in your documents. Stated more simply, two out of nine board members cannot make a decision that is binding on an association. Instead, on a nine-member board, at least five members (the quorum number) need to be present and accounted for to even *discuss* issues related to the community.

How does this come into play? In several ways. First, as we've noted, you can't hold a legal board meeting without a quorum. So if the board was to decide anything at a meeting where a quorum was not present, that decision would be invalid. Hundreds of judges around the country have had to invalidate board decisions because of quorum violations. Second, any time a quorum of directors discusses an issue related to the association, that discussion is considered a board meeting—and if that meeting was not noticed and open to owners, it was illegal. So it is not OK for a few directors to chat about insurance while sitting by the pool. That does not mean that a quorum of board members can never gather together at dinner parties and social events; it simply means that association business cannot be discussed there.

In many states, the quorum and notice requirements apply not only to boards but also to executive committees—especially when those committees have been delegated decision-making power or are discussing finances. So a board cannot circumvent the rules by establishing a committee of its members to discuss an issue privately. However, there is a clever workaround: the committee of one. If a committee only has a single member, it never has to meet, and therefore the concepts of notice and quorum become irrelevant. Still, this is probably the least representative situation possible, so it should be used sparingly; it may be reasonable to have a one-member beautification committee, but a one-person insurance committee would be a poor idea except, perhaps, in a brand-new community with limited owner participation.

Fifty years ago quorum rules weren't all that difficult to follow. Conference calls were uncommon, and e-mail hadn't been invented. It wasn't really possible for a board to discuss an issue without meeting in person. Today, however, technology allows for rampant violation of basic corporate procedure. It is not at all unusual for a board to operate largely via e-mail, reasoning that the directors are not actually "meeting" but simply communicating individually, en masse. This may sound reasonable, but in fact there's no question that mass e-mail messages and conference calls involving a quorum of members *do* constitute a board meeting, and that casual decisions made in this way are not proper. It is OK to discuss an issue with fewer than a quorum of board members. It is even OK to hold several simultaneous electronic discussions with different small groups of board members. If you want to follow the letter of the law, however, the minute that more than a quorum of members is on the same e-mail distribution list, you have a problem.

There is, however, a positive flip side to this issue: A quorum *can* be established by conference call. Even an absentee board can hold completely legal meetings using telephone conferencing to establish a quorum and discuss association business—just make certain that at least one board member is at the home base so the meeting can be open to residents. Alternatively, you can open the conference bridge to all residents, but that quickly becomes both chaotic and prohibitively expensive.

We've established that all meetings of a quorum of board members must be properly noticed and open to residents. But what exactly does *open* mean? Is an open meeting a free-for-all where any person is allowed to spout off on any issue ad nauseam, until the rest of the owners are driven to tears?

Enter parliamentary procedure, which is used to enforce decorum. Every meeting must have a chairperson, and usually that person is the president. The chairperson is responsible for establishing the order of business and deciding what issues are discussed, based on the agenda that was noticed to owners. An open meeting does *not* mean that any owner may speak for any amount of time on any issue. (In fact, while member participation is practically universal in condominiums, it is not necessarily common in HOAs—so while HOA meetings must almost always be "open," the members may or may not be allowed to speak.) Instead, proper procedure allows the chairperson to limit comments to a reasonable time frame, and he or she may disallow comments that are not relevant to the issue being discussed. Many statutes and documents provide the appropriate rules about whether owners must be allowed to speak and about the minimum time frame (usually just a few minutes).

Now, assume that a meeting has been organized and noticed. The board has achieved a quorum and discussed an issue, and the directors are ready to vote. A motion is made and seconded, and comments have been closed. Next it's time to canvass the votes—figure out who is voting which way. Most votes must be open and public. Generally, board members vote by show of hands or by voice. The presiding officer will say something similar to "All those in favor of the motion, say aye," and they will; then the officer will say, "Those against?" and those members speak up—just like you've seen in movies. The count is tallied, and the vote either passes or fails. Simple.

Some communities might ask for written ballots on an issue, and then will read these out loud (along with the name of the person casting the vote). However, the board must be careful that these are not *secret* ballots, which are almost never allowed during board meetings. Everyone is entitled to know how board members vote—this is a basic principle of representative democracy. A secret ballot vote precludes the community members from knowing how well their elected directors are serving them according to fiduciary duty. In fact, the only situation where secret ballots may be allowed is during director elections—other than that, every board decision (save those exempted from the public meeting requirements, such as legal strategy discussions) must be open and obvious.

Does everyone have to vote? Not necessarily. An *abstention* occurs when a board member chooses not to vote for or against an issue. Under some laws, board members are not allowed to abstain unless there is a conflict of interest (some form of financial entanglement or perhaps a familial relationship). But other laws allow board members to abstain under any circumstances, for any reason. Basically, an abstention is a way for board members to punt their decision to the other members and absolve themselves of their decision-making responsibility. Doesn't sound like a good thing? That's because it's not—and generally a director should never abstain from voting unless there is a genuine conflict, no matter what the law allows. That way, board members cannot foist their duties—and the liability for any failures—onto the other members.

In addition to providing notice, establishing a quorum, and voting, a board of directors has a responsibility to keep *minutes* of the meeting. The minutes are a semidetailed record of the entire process, including the time of the meeting, the call to order, the order of business, general notes on discussion, the specific outcome of votes, and the actions taken. It is not necessary to transcribe the meeting word for word, as a court reporter would. Instead, it is OK simply to state that an issue was discussed and to indicate the result of the vote. Usually the secretary is responsible for keeping the meeting minutes, but sometimes the property manager can take on the task.

MEMBERSHIP MEETINGS

A number of decisions in a community association must be made not by the board of directors alone but by the membership at large. One obvious example would be elections (it would be difficult for the board to elect itself), but there are a number of other common situations, including amendments to the documents, modification of certain vested rights, consideration of material alterations or capital expenditures, collection of reserves, and exercising the owner's right to recall the board.

All these tasks are handled at a *membership meeting*. Most associations will hold at least one annual membership meeting, primarily to conduct elections. There may also be any number of special membership meetings, depending on whether there are other membershipwide issues to discuss. However, as for board meetings, membership meetings must satisfy quorum requirements (at least 50 percent plus one) before business may be conducted. Think for a moment about how hard it is to get a group of five or ten people together in one place at the same time. Now assume that your association has three hundred units. That means you'll need 151 unit owners present simply to conduct business! Not to mention that many of the tasks you hope to achieve require a positive vote much higher than a simple quorum—often up to 75 percent. How could this ever possibly occur?

The sad truth is, many hundreds of community associations around the country have never once held a successful membership meeting. The owners are simply too spread out, or too disinterested, to participate in their home government. The process of establishing a quorum is by itself a Herculean task. Many a new association has spent hours planning a raft of positive amendments to the documents, only to find that those amendments can never be voted upon. It's a sad fact of association life, but it's one that many owners have to deal with. Recognizing this difficulty, the Uniform Act provides that 20 percent may satisfy a quorum at a membership meeting, and 50 percent at a board meeting. However, it is extremely likely that even in Uniform Act states, a community's documents require a higher percentage.

The rules of procedure do give associations a strong weapon to combat disinterest and malaise: a *proxy*. A proxy is a person who is given the right to vote on your behalf. Generally, that person is the secretary of the association, but you can specify any person you want, whether or not that person is another unit owner. So if you can't attend a meeting in person, you simply designate a proxy (using a proxy form), and that person will attend the meeting for you. How does the proxy know how to vote in your interest? Well, there are two types of proxies. The first, a *general proxy*, allows you to designate unlimited voting power to another person, who will make all the decisions. However, you give a *limited proxy* (sometimes called an *instructed proxy*) only the power to vote exactly how you want on each specific issue to be discussed at the meeting—like a ballot, except in the form of a person.

So why not simply use ballots to vote on *all* questions that arise before the membership? Because, except in elections, ballots cannot satisfy the quorum requirement. There have to actually be people at the meeting, in person, to constitute a legal gathering for voting purposes. In an election, however, most laws do in fact allow the votes to occur by ballot, and even with an extremely low number of residents voting (sometimes as low as 20 percent), the election is legal. This compromise simply acknowledges the reality: If half of the association members were required to participate in elections, one might never be held, and no one would ever run the association. It's a vicious circle.

As with a board meeting, any membership meetings must be noticed—but the time frames are far more conservative. You can assume that at least fourteen days' notice is required for most meetings, and much more for elections (which have different time frames for submitting nominations, preparing platforms, and then sending in the ballots).

Also as with a board meeting, someone is required to run the proceedings—a single chairperson designated in your bylaws. This is often the association president, for reasons of convenience, but a new chairperson can be designated or elected at any time before the meeting. Remember, a membership meeting is not a board meeting, and it doesn't need to be handled like one. The board members have no particular role relating to their service as directors. While it is common at membership meetings for the directors to sit at the front of the room, this is unnecessary. At a membership meeting, the board members are equal to every other owner. They have one vote and no special powers.

A membership meeting is a unique opportunity for the members to make certain decisions that only they are allowed to make. Votes will be taken just like at a board meeting, with owners voting out loud or by hand, and then any proxies voting en masse as well. Again, every vote must be open, because everyone is entitled to know how their neighbor is voting. There are no secrets in SOC government.

In summary, because an SOC is run by a group of elected volunteers, the actions they take must be made during open meetings, after adequate notice has been provided to the other members.

These meetings are conducted using the ordinary rules of procedure familiar to any organization. Sometimes, the membership at large will meet to discuss issues, and these member meetings operate according to established procedural rules as well.

Now that you understand how to get together and make decisions without killing each other, we're going to talk about the basic rights granted to every unit owner—and the responsibilities that go along with that unbridled power.

IT'S YOUR PARTY
(UNIT OWNER RIGHTS AND RESPONSIBILITIES)

In the preceding chapters, we've discussed how unit owners must give up some autonomy to satisfy the needs of the common good, and how the requisite duties of community living affect your every-day life. However, don't assume that you're buying a piece of paper and a mud hut. Unit owners in SOCs have a very significant quiver of rights they can access to ensure that they are treated fairly, that their investment is protected, and that their basic right to reasonable governance is recognized.

In general, the rights granted to unit owners are all about *oversight*. We've discussed the fact that a community association is most efficiently run by an elected body of representatives, who then make decisions, consistent with their role as fiduciaries, that protect the property and its value. That's the *balance*—but as always, a *check* is needed to ensure that the board members and officers do their jobs properly, and that they can be removed from office if that is not the case. The inalienable rights of unit owners provide a very significant set of checks against abuse, unfair dealings, and basic incompetence. These various rights—to vote, to receive notice, to assemble, to access association books and records, to use common elements, to sell or rent your unit—are in place to ensure that your representatives are doing their job.

VOTING

Perhaps the defining characteristic of democracy is the process of voting—the casting of ballots to determine by majority which candidates will represent the citizens. If you have the right to do one thing in your association, it's to vote. As soon as your deed is recorded in the public records, the right to vote on behalf of your unit automatically transfers to you, and you are immediately able to participate.

That said, not every unit has the right to vote—your documents will specify exactly which units have a voting interest and, in some cases, how many interests they hold. Many SOCs that include nonresidential property, such as storage units, do not grant extra voting rights to owners of those units; individual state law will specify whether this is the case. But these associations may grant a "weighted" vote in the form of extra interests to larger units, on the assumption that those units have a greater financial stake in the association. Whatever the situation in your SOC, you can be assured that those voting units can never be amended without the unanimous vote of the owners, because that is a basic, vested contractual right. Whatever vote you have already, you have for perpetuity—and whatever you don't have, you're not going to get.

Another form of slanted voting, one that has been largely banned, is called *cumulative voting.* When there are three board positions to be filled, each unit therefore has three votes to cast—one for each vacancy. Cumulative voting is when a single unit casts all three votes for the same candidate. In this fashion, a candidate could have a plurality of votes but the results would not in fact represent a majority of unit owners. You can see why this concept, which flies in the face of true representation, is generally prohibited.

The most common voting situation in any association is the election of the board of directors, which typically occurs on an annual basis. As we mentioned earlier, a number of states have created very specific rules for elections, down to the size of the envelopes that must be mailed to owners. In general, your association will solicit nominations for candidates, send out ballots to all owners, and then count those ballots at a membership meeting. The candidates with the most votes will serve on the board—just like high school.

The election process has a significant enemy, however: apathy. You may notice that your state statute specifies an extremely small number of ballots for a legal election to have occurred—perhaps 20 percent of all owners. That's because, in many communities, it's unrealistic for more than that number of unit owners to participate. If only 20 percent of your neighbors have voted, the elected board is not very representative. But that's not the fault of the state, or the association, or the directors. It's the fault of the apathetic owners. You have an inalienable right to vote—make sure you exercise that right. It's the only way you can be represented in your community government. The second head of the apathy monster is the dearth of candidates who offer themselves for the job. It's not uncommon to have uncontested elections in SOCs—and in these situations the vote is meaningless. So not only do you have a right to vote, but you may also have a duty to consider serving your association by running for office.

Voting and serving as an elected representative—these are basic principles of citizenship. Without sacrifice, there is no reward. No one is asking you to lay your life on the line—although in some contentious communities, it may seem that way.[1] But if you have the time and wherewithal to help guide your association, you should seriously consider throwing your hat in the ring.

In addition to voting for your board of directors, you may also have the right to vote on a number of other issues that affect your community. For example, amendments to the documents will almost always require a vote of owners, and usually a very significant percentage (as high as 75 percent) must agree before an amendment is adopted. But because of the apathy monster, you can assume that all but the most basic or important amendments may be difficult to achieve.

Some states (for example, those that use the Uniform Laws) also allow a majority of owners to reject the annual budget. While this seems like a great idea, it may pose some difficulties in practice. Remember that unlike the directors, who have a legal duty to act in the best interests of the members of the association, the members at large are under no such obligation. When one hundred or more uninformed unit owners, each with his or her own agenda, votes on a budget that affects the entire community, it can often produce inappropriate results. It's notable that even the AARP, which by nature

---

1 In Arizona, on April 19, 2000, a unit owner killed two directors at a board meeting, citing perceived wrongs that he believed had been committed against him by the association. Stories like this may be rare, but they do exist.

errs on the side of protecting unit-owner rights, does not argue that owners as a whole should be approving association budgets.[2]

So while you have the right to vote, it is often unwieldy at best. Is there no oversight, then? What can unit owners in an SOC do about a board gone wild, spending money on Swarovski crystal welcome mats, diamond elevator emblems, and original Picassos? What if the board truly doesn't represent the community or its best interests? As we touched upon in the previous chapter, unit owners wield the ultimate hammer, and it's called *recall*. At any time, a majority of unit owners may vote to remove any or all of the board members, for any or no reason, and replace them with candidates who better represent their needs. What more powerful weapon could there be to assert your rights?

Recall is not always all it's cracked up to be, however. It's not uncommon for a unit owner to attempt the organization of a recall, only to find either that he or she is in a distinct minority, or that the majority of owners aren't interested enough in the community to take action. While you and your best friends may feel that the association needs to ban children from the hot tub, that doesn't mean your other neighbors agree. Unfortunately, nothing infuriates motivated owners more than to find that they are in the minority among their neighbors—and an owner who organizes an unsuccessful recall will likely be an enemy of that board for years to come.

Think for a moment about your neighbors and how much their lifestyles differ. You all have legitimate issues and concerns, but your ideas are often simply not compatible with one another. And it's up to the board of directors to sift through these demands and run the association in a manner that is consistent with their primary

---

2 Many residents are incorrect in believing that their state statutes do not allow associations to raise their maintenance more than a certain percentage in a single year. More often, the actual statute simply gives owners the right to present an alternative budget to the board. But because the board has a legal responsibility to budget for 100 percent of the association's expenses, such laws are somewhat oxymoronic.

goals: protecting the common property and enforcing the covenants. Now you see why serving on a board is a tough, sometimes thankless job. So the next time you meet a board member, give him a hug. He probably needs one.

NOTICE AND ASSEMBLY

We've already discussed notice—the fact that, in general, board meetings and membership meetings are open to all unit owners, and that those owners must be given sufficient notice of the meeting to enable them to attend and participate (though not always verbally). In addition to this, owners have a broader right to assemble with their neighbors in whatever manner they choose, to discuss any issues they like. The board cannot prevent you from meeting with a cadre of other disenchanted owners to discuss its demise, just as it cannot prevent you from holding your bridge game in the clubroom.

However, the association may impose reasonable time, place, and manner restrictions—for example, no parties after 10:00 p.m., and no blocking the entrance with a picket line.[3] It may also be able to restrict commercial activities on the property. But you have a right to assemble on your own property with other owners for any reason—so long as it's legal. For example, your right of assembly doesn't give you the right to slander people, even those who serve on the board. They are not public figures, and they will sue you if you sit in the lobby with placards calling them thieving imbeciles. (Of course, if they are *actually* stealing, you'll probably win your lawsuit—but why take the risk? Better to go to the police than to take the law into your own hands.)

---

3 In what might be considered an extreme example, one condominium association decided to ban visitors after 11 p.m., citing security concerns. After that time, any car parked in a visitor spot is towed away.

Similarly, while the directors have the right to limit comments at board meetings, they certainly don't have the right to limit discussion at other times. In one condominium, a dictatorial, clearly out-of-control board of directors stormed into a dinner party being held by dissatisfied owners and declared that any issues affecting the community could only be discussed at a board meeting. Of course, that's complete balderdash—you have every right to talk to people whenever you wish, no matter the subject.

ACCESS TO THE BOOKS AND RECORDS

Community associations are corporate-style entities, and as such their files are made available to every shareholder or unit owner. You have the right to access at least some of the books and records of the association (exactly which documents depends on the laws of your state) in order to oversee its expenditures, read through its communications, and generally nose through the business of running the property. Naturally, there are some limitations. First, documents prepared for litigation (such as attorney-client communications) are never available to residents, because to reveal these would be to violate the confidentiality privilege between attorneys and their clients. Second, while the association must allow you to access the documents, it may ask that you make an appointment to do so and that you pay for any photocopies you make (which is only reasonable). Other than that, if you want to sit in the management office for days, reading through e-mail, that's your right—and it provides owners with the ultimate oversight.

For example, it's extremely common for owners to ask the basic question "Where does all the money go?" Do you really want to know? Then head down to the office and request a copy of the current budget—which, by the way, the association probably sent to you when it was being considered, and then again when it was approved. (Many states even mandate sending an annual audit or a financial report to owners—which you probably tossed promptly in the garbage.) You can also ask to look at all the invoices that have been received and all the checks that have been written. The association will have kept a copy of these documents—often for many years, depending on the requirements of your particular state.

You are also allowed to access a list of owners, their addresses, their current telephone numbers, and possibly their e-mail addresses. That means if you want to contact your neighbors to try to oust the board members, they can't stop you from doing so. (But neither can they stop other realtor-owners from sending solicitation letters to all their neighbors, or contractors from sending out advertisements. That's just one of the negative effects of a completely open system.)

Notwithstanding rules that allow open access, there are a number of types of information that may typically be withheld from inspection. These include:

- Medical records (generally used to support a disability claim or the need for a reasonable accommodation or modification)
- Contracts that are currently in negotiation
- Pending or potential litigation
- Administrative proceedings regarding enforcement of the declaration or bylaws (although sometimes settlement agreements may not be kept confidential)
- Privileged communications
- Information that is protected by law (like Social Security numbers)
- Individual unit files other than those of the requesting owner

Other than these examples, as long as you are not disruptive and do not interfere with the management of the property, you gener-

ally have the right to become informed about your community. Use
it wisely!

USE OF THE COMMON ELEMENTS

In Chapter 1 we explained that, in addition to owning your unit,
you also own an undivided interest in the common elements and
common areas—so it stands to reason that, as a unit owner, you
have a vested, appurtenant right to use those facilities. If you own
a unit, you can use the common property. Of course, as always, a
few restrictions apply.

First, the association is entitled to establish reasonable time
restrictions to enhance safety or to avoid nuisance to other residents. If the association deems it necessary to close the gym after
11:00 p.m., it has the right to do so. While you do own the common
areas, you also share them with hundreds of others—and this is one
of those situations where the needs of the community may outweigh
your own. If you're a late-night gym rat, you may have to invest in
a Bowflex.

Second, and related, you can't use the property in a manner that
hinders the rights of other unit owners. For example, it's not OK
to set up a bounce house for your child's birthday party so that it
blocks a main road. In fact, you may be unable to hold an exclusive
party in the common areas under any circumstances. The association may decide to allow unit owners to reserve an area for an
exclusive use (such as a party), generally for a small fee, but it is
in no way required to do so. Swimming pools are always a great
example of this principle. While you may want to hold your wedding under the gazebo at your oceanfront condominium, the association has no obligation to restrict the other owners from watching
the festivities or even using the pool. So be prepared: Your dream

wedding may be attended by wet toddlers, rowdy teenagers, and thonged European bathers.

Finally, while an association generally does not have the power to ban you from using the common elements, some states now allow buildings to deny the use of *certain* common elements (such as the pool) if unit owners have not paid their maintenance. This rule is extremely variable, so check your own state law.

SELLING OR RENTING

If you live in a cooperative, you might as well skip this section, because your rights to alienate your unit are extremely abbreviated. But other property owners generally enjoy the right, with relatively minor restrictions, to sell or rent their property.

The sale element is a no-brainer. Permission to transfer your interest to another person is a fundamental principle of property ownership. If you can't sell it, than you don't really own the property. No association in any state can entirely *prevent* you from selling your unit.

That said, associations can apply a few restrictions that may reduce your ability to alienate your property. Perhaps the most common is the *right of first refusal* (often called the *preemptive right*). Many association documents say that the association has first dibs on the purchase of any unit at the agreed-upon, contractual sale price. So you do get to sell your property—but possibly not to the person who first accepted the deal. Why would an association want to purchase a unit in the development? For the same reason anyone would—because it's a good investment. Let's assume that the real-estate market is in the toilet and units are selling for well below market value. It may be in the best interests of the association to purchase a unit in hopes that, several years later, it can sell the property at a significant profit (and reduce maintenance costs in the process).

Of course, this introduces the issue of risk, and there are a lot of homeowners who believe that their association should never be engaging in speculation of any kind. But an aversion to risk taking can be its own type of risk. Buy low, sell high—it works in the stock market, and it works in real estate. Put it this way: If you believe in your property, and if the board doesn't have the right to purchase properties at a below-market rate, you should be doing so personally.

The second most common restriction on alienation is a ban on financing greater than a certain percentage of a unit's value. Because an association relies on income from owners, it therefore has a strong interest in ensuring that any new members can pay their fair share. More important, if you're leveraged to the hilt and have no equity in your unit, you are far less likely to be able to restore it after a potential disaster. Your unit would remain a vacant drain on the rebuilt property until it is sold or foreclosed. Associations thrive on a community of financially stable, insured owners who can afford their investment, whether that investment is a mobile home or a palatial estate.

RIGHT TO A VIEW

It is pretty universally believed that when you buy property with an unfettered view of your surroundings, you have the right to keep it that way. Why would you pay a premium for a lakefront estate if you couldn't guarantee a continued view of the lake? And yet in many states, there is no such right. If the association owns the property between you and your view, and if it decides to landscape, you're out of luck. You can always plead your case at a board meeting, but remember that there are hundreds of other association members, and it's likely that none of them care if you can see the lake—they're pleased that the vacant lot has been turned into a park. So never assume that you have any particular right to see anything from your unit.

Similarly, you generally don't have the right to prevent your neighbors from blocking your view, either. When the homeowner next door decides to enhance his privacy with a row of lush elm trees, and your living room window now looks out onto a forest, there's nothing you can do. That's just the risk you take in an HOA. You can control your own property, but not your neighbor's—unless the documents provide otherwise.

Perhaps the most common view-blocking situation occurs in high-rise buildings, when construction starts on the mammoth condominium tower in the open lot next door. You bought an ocean view unit, but now you own a condo that's just *near* the ocean. There's no way to ensure that your view won't be blocked someday—unless your windows look directly onto the ocean, and your own association owns all the property that might potentially restrict your view. Even then, if the community decides to build a clubhouse on that open land, you may have to prepare yourself for a battle royal against the board of directors.

What follows is a list of the most common unit owner rights. Not all of them are universal, but it's likely that these rights will be granted to you by statute, by common law, or in your documents.

1. A purchaser has a right to receive a complete set of condominium documents as well as disclosure documents from the developer, and to rescind the contract to purchase at any time within a set number of days from receipt of all required documents.

2. A new condominium unit comes with an implied warranty of fitness and merchantability, as well as a common-law implied warranty that the unit will be constructed using sound workmanship in accordance with the approved building plans and code specifications.

3. A unit owner is entitled to the exclusive possession of his or her unit.

4. Unit owners and their invited guests are entitled to use the common elements, common areas, and recreational facilities that serve the condominium, in accordance with the purposes for which they are intended, but no use may hinder or encroach upon the lawful rights of other unit owners.

5. Unit owners often have the right to invite candidates for public office to appear and speak in and around the common elements, common areas, and recreational facilities, subject to reasonable rules adopted by the association.

6. Unit owners have the right to peaceably assemble in and around the common elements, common areas, and recreational facilities.

7. All owners have a right of access to any available franchised or licensed cable television service and, pursuant to the Telecommunications Act of 1996, to install a satellite dish on property exclusively owned or controlled by the unit owner (learn more about this in Chapter 12).

8. Unit owners have a right to receive thirty days' notice of an alleged delinquency before the board initiates a foreclosure on a lien that would secure the obligation owed to the association. (This right is left up to the states, but the statutes are all relatively similar.)

9. The association is prohibited from changing a unit owner's share of the common elements, voting rights, or unit appurtenances without the unit owner's written consent.

10. A unit owner has the right of peaceful possession of the unit, free from unwarranted nuisances. (You can't cause them, but you don't have to suffer them, either.)

11. Unit owners have the right to notice, with a posted agenda, of board and membership meetings, and they may also have the right to speak about items on the agenda.

12. Unit owners may have the right to audio record and videotape meetings of the board and membership meetings.

13. Unit owners have the right to notice of and attendance at meetings of committees that take final action on behalf of the board or that make recommendations to the board regarding association budget issues, as well as all other committee meetings unless excluded by an amendment to the condominium documents.

14. Unit owners have the right to inspect a copy of each insurance policy in effect.

15. Unit owners have the right to inspect the official records of the association and to make or obtain copies of these records. The right of record inspection is subject to reasonable rules of the association regarding the frequency, time, location, nature, and manner of record inspections and copying.

16. Depending on the state, every unit owner may have the right to receive a complete financial report of actual receipts and expenditures for the previous twelve months, either annually or within sixty days following the end of the fiscal or calendar year.

17. Unit owners have a right to maintain a warranty action.

18. A unit owner has the right to receive personal notice of any board meeting where the board will consider nonemergency assessments or rules regarding unit use.

19. Unit owners have the right to elect and recall the board at any time, with or without cause.

20. In situations where the condominium documents grant the board fining authority, before a fine can be levied unit owners have the right to notice of the alleged violation of the covenants or the rules and regulations, an opportunity to cure the violation, and a hearing.

21. Unit owners have a right to qualify for (and serve on) the board.

22. Unit owners are entitled to notice of any special assessment, including the specific purpose for the collection.

So you have rights—but do you get them for free? In exchange for all these rights, you also have a number of *responsibilities*. They're simple, but for many people they're not worth the cost of ownership. You should understand them before you get involved in community living. We discuss these issues in various other chapters, but here is a summary:

- You have an obligation to abide by the covenants, restrictions, rules, and regulations. They're not optional, they're mandatory. Follow them.

- You must pay your proportionate share of the common expenses and any special assessments. A condominium is not an apartment building. You can't withhold "rent" in protest of some association policy. If you don't pay your maintenance, the association will file a lien against your property, and then it will foreclose on that lien. The community cannot operate without assessments, so courts are very strict in enforcing them.

- You cannot create nuisances that disturb your neighbors. These include smells, smoke, noises—anything that affects your neighbors' quiet enjoyment of their own units. We've devoted Chapter 11 entirely to the concept of nuisance.

- You may have a duty (even mandated by some state laws) to carry casualty and liability insurance. If your property is not insured, it is that much more likely that it will be abandoned after a disaster.
- You can't modify the common elements (whether limited or no) without approval of the board or, possibly, the other unit owners. That means you're not allowed to replace your windows with stained glass just because it suits your fancy.

And basically, that's all there is. You have a laundry list of rights and very few responsibilities. Actually, it's an extremely fair system, very heavily weighted toward unit owners. Not too bad a deal!

In summary, as a member of a mandatory association you have certain responsibilities (such as paying your maintenance), but you also have a number of rights, including the right to vote, to inspect the corporate documents, to participate in meetings and elections, and to sell or rent your property. You have to admit, that's a pretty good list! However, you may want to grab a pack of antacids (or even a Valium) before we begin the next chapter, which deals with finances: How do associations pay the bills, and how much of the tab is your responsibility?

FOR THE LOVE OF MONEY
(BUDGETING AND FINANCE)

Money makes the world go round, but it's also the root of all evil. It can't buy you happiness or love, but it talks—and in SOCs, it talks loudly. Even more than power or lifestyle issues, financial matters are at the core of most association battles.

Generally in life one rule holds steady: If it looks like a duck and quacks like a duck, it's probably a duck. But that principle doesn't work when it comes to SOCs. Because while they may look like private homes and seem like private homes, in reality they're businesses, and they need to be run accordingly. Unlike a private home, your community is likely to have multiple employees, both management-level and hourly workers; a security system; comprehensive insurance, including workers' compensation and D&O liability; large utility bills; legal issues; engineering issues; and hundreds of owners, all of whom think that they know how to run the association better than anyone else. But that's almost never true; there's a wide disparity between managing your household accounts and managing a business. And, as a business, any SOC runs on its lifeblood: assessments. If you cut off the blood flow as a result of the board's failure to do its job or the unit owners' failure to pay their fair share, the community will die.

We've already discussed who gets to run the association—a board of elected representatives, along with a smaller number of elected or appointed officers. And we've explained that these representatives have pledged the unit owners a fiduciary duty to maintain the common elements—a duty not held by the members at large. The question is, how do they get the money they need to operate the association? Who pays the bills?

You do. You and all your neighbors. The association is responsible for the maintenance, repair, and replacement of the common elements. And the Uniform Act (along with other laws) provides that all common expenses must be assessed against all the units, in accordance with the allocations set forth in each community's documents. So the board has an obligation both to maintain the common property and to pass those costs onto the owners.[1] As a purchaser of a unit in an SOC you must come to terms with the reality that, as an owner, you are responsible for your share of the common expenses, regardless of how high those expenses might be—and you cannot

---

1 A number of states take this principle a step further, by requiring that the assessments collected are sufficient to cover 100 percent of the costs of maintaining the association. Essentially, it's a balanced-budget policy—the directors cannot present a budget that undercollects funds, even if they know that they will specially assess for the shortfall later on.

escape that reality by asserting your disinterest in the amenities or by pleading your personal financial difficulties.

But how does the board decide how much to charge each owner? Just like any corporation, finance starts with a budget. Each year, the board of directors is obligated to prepare and present a budget that estimates the total expenses for the year, based on historical averages and the board's best judgment. Sometimes, the directors will create a finance committee that is tasked with drafting the budget and presenting it to the board for approval. At other times, the job is left to the treasurer or perhaps even the property manager. But at some point, someone has to actually sit down and examine each expenditure category and try to determine how much money the association needs to do its job.

That's not always an easy task. For one thing, new associations have very little history on which to base an educated guess. While developers are required to create estimated operational budgets as part of the prospectus, those budgets are often severely *underestimated*, primarily because they are prepared years before the development is sold (so they do not take all factors into consideration). Some developers may even purposely lowball the estimated budget in order to make the economics of owning a unit more attractive to prospective buyers. Even in established communities, it's possible that world events will have substantially changed the cost of services since the prior year. War in the Middle East? Better plan a bit more for oil and gas. Hurricane wiped out half of Georgia? You can expect your windstorm insurance to double—assuming you can find an insurer who will underwrite the policy.

Further complicating the issue, especially when it comes to pleasing the other unit owners, is the fact that SOC insurance, banking, and utility options differ substantially from those of a private home. When you shop for household insurance, it's probable that you will have a dozen different options from which you can shop for the best rate. But high-rise buildings, especially in coastal areas, aren't so lucky. It's not uncommon for there to be only a single insurance company willing to insure the property, and then at an exorbitant rate—and the association is generally obligated to secure that policy. Similarly, while you may be getting 5 percent interest on the $20,000 you have sitting in a money market, banks don't always allow corporations to save in the same fashion. The association may have hundreds of thousands of dollars, but unless a bank is willing to bypass the FDIC limit and personally insure such a large account, these savings will need to be spread among dozens of banks—and the operating account often does not pay interest.

Finally, the preparation of a budget, just like the management of the association, requires following a decision-making process—and there's no way that every resident will agree with every board decision. The board is obligated to maintain the common elements, but at what level? Does that require window cleaning once a year or three times a year? How often should the lawn be mown? How many hours of housekeeping are required each week? Should the building turn off the lights at night? Are fresh flowers needed in the lobby, or are silk plants sufficient? There's no single answer to any of these questions. To a large extent, the budget will depend upon the makeup of the property and the lifestyle to which the unit owners are accustomed. In principle, the board has been elected by a majority of voters, so the decisions it makes should represent the will of the majority. Of course, that's not always how it works out.

Furthermore, there's always a small group of owners who have unusual (and sometimes illegal) plans for saving money—usually at any cost. Why can't we let the public use our pool, and charge them an access fee? Why don't we turn off the hot water at night? Can we get the owners to clean the lobby instead of housekeepers? Do we really need insurance? And so on. People run their own lives in different ways, and consequently they have different ideas of how to operate the association that manages their home life.

This is why, ultimately, the question of budgeting is very contentious and often incites anger. Budget time is one of the most unpleasant times of the year for any board member. Everyone likes to eat dinner, but no one likes to get the bill.

In addition to the everyday expenses, a number of states require the association to collect a *reserve*. Reserve funds are monies set aside for long-term repair and replacement of the physical structures—such as the roof, the concrete, and the mechanical systems—and for protection against common contingencies. The association hires an appraiser who analyzes the common elements, determines the remaining lifespan, estimates the costs of eventually replacing the worn structures, and divides that into an annual amount. This money is then squirreled away for a rainy day, so that when the roof ultimately needs to be replaced, it doesn't require a huge special assessment of funds.

In states where a reserve is mandatory, unit owners must be assessed for their share of the reserve *in addition to* the other costs of maintaining the property. Even in these states, if the association wants to skip the reserve, it can do so—but only with a majority vote of the owners, and only if that vote is repeated every single year. A few cases currently floating around in the court system suggest that regardless of statutory regulation, failing to collect a reserve is a breach of an association's fiduciary duty; when the decisions are eventually handed down, this questionable practice likely will be an option no longer.

The government already tries to make it difficult to skip out on the reserves, because these funds are crucial to financial stability in the long term. A smart buyer will always check whether an SOC has a fully funded reserve; if it does not, you can be sure that the total costs of large repairs will ultimately come out of your own pocket. A unit in a building with a reserve fund is a safer investment than a similar unit in a building that has waived collection for years. So even if your state doesn't mandate a statutory reserve, it's in the best interests of any SOC to begin one of its own. And if your state does require a reserve, don't vote to waive it—at least not completely. It's a very shortsighted decision that may save you some money today but certainly will cost you in the long run. There are other, better ways than waiving your reserve fund to handle your finances wisely.

Budgets, like community documents, are not written in stone. If, as the year goes by, it becomes clear that the association has underbudgeted significantly in one area, it can shift funds from overbudgeted categories, keeping the original budget in balance. Or the board can amend the budget and collect more money from the owners. Alternatively, the board can approve a *special assessment* for the sole purpose of correcting that shortfall.

ASSESSMENTS

So an annual budget has been approved by your board of directors or by the membership at large (as discussed in Chapter 8). How does the association determine your share of the funds, and how does it collect? By a procedure known as *assessment*.

Traditionally, there have been two methods by which an association may divide the common expenses: Either every unit pays an equal share, or each pays a percent share (pro rata) based on the square footage of the unit in relation to other units. The Uniform Act, however, presents developers with the option of dividing the units using *any* formula, as long as it's consistent (based on cost of the unit, for example, or the predicted cost of utilities). In any case, once the developer chooses a method and writes it into the documents, it cannot be changed without a 100 percent vote of the owners (and usually all lien holders of record as well). The question of which system is fair is likely to divide the association directly down the middle. Owners of larger units, naturally, would prefer that the division be equal, and owners of small units want to pay only their share. But when you bought your unit, you were informed of the division, and it will never be changed. So it is what it is.

After passing the annual budget, the association determines your share of the funds required for operations and then bills you regularly—usually each month (although quarterly collections are common in HOAs, where the common expenses tend to be far less than in a condominium). This charge is generally called *maintenance* because the funds are used to maintain the property.

It's very important to point out once again that maintenance is not the same as rent. There are no situations in which you can legally withhold a valid maintenance assessment—not if you hate the board, not if it's mismanaging the association, not if your roof leaks like a colander. If you feel your board isn't doing its job, you can either sue the association or attempt to organize a recall. In the meantime, you must pay your maintenance each and every month.[2]

In addition to monthly assessments, SOCs will often need to collect what is known as a *special assessment*. This is just what it sounds like—an assessment of funds to be used for a single and special purpose that was not anticipated in the annual budget. But why would a special assessment ever be required? If the board members have

---

2 Technically, an owner can withhold payment of an assessment that is levied illegally—for example, if the board authorized a large construction project without holding a proper meeting. As a practical matter, however, the association will simply put a lien on any property that does not pay, and the owner will then be forced to fight the lien in court. The better strategy would be to pay the assessment and then challenge it in a separate lawsuit. That does add an extra wrinkle, however: Even if the action taken is unauthorized, and even if the owner wins the case, the cost of defending against the lawsuit (as well as any payments required to undo the board action) would be a legitimate cost of business, and therefore the board may assess all owners to collect those expenses.

done their jobs properly, wouldn't every expense be anticipated in the budget? In some associations, the board includes a "contingency" line item in the budget to be used for emergency expenditures—and this will cover a lot of random occurrences. But unless the association is going to collect hundreds of thousands of extra dollars each year, special assessments will inevitably be required. The most common cause of a special assessment involves insurance deductibles. Even if your property carries insurance, there is likely to be a substantial deductible. With windstorm insurance, that deductible can run into the millions. So any disaster or hazard that strikes the property, whether it be fire or flood, wind or earthquake, is going to require a significant outlay of funds before insurance begins to pay. That money will be collected in a special assessment.

The second most common situation involves upgrades and repairs. Eventually, any property will deteriorate. Furniture is going to tear, floors will get worn down, and paint and wallpaper become stained and faded. These types of expenses are not necessarily covered by a reserve account. So when it's time for the association to update the lobby, the only way to pay for the remodeling is to specially assess owners for the cost. And remember, it's the responsibility of the board to maintain the common elements. This includes making sure that they're not worn out beyond repair; when a board delays a repair to shift the cost to a later date (known as *deferred maintenance*), the later repair is almost always more expensive than if it had been fixed in a timely manner.

A third special assessment often levied by associations is for litigation expenses, especially for turnover litigation. A full-on trial could cost anywhere from $200,000 to $500,000 to litigate, and legal fees are generally not recoverable in construction lawsuits. Unless the board has stashed away half a million dollars somewhere in the budget, this is a cost that will require a special assessment.

Another common special assessment concerns bad debt. Ultimately there's a certain amount of overdue maintenance in any association that will never be repaid—even if you lien the property or threaten to foreclose. Like any other business, some money owed to the association will never be collected. This uncollectible money is called *bad debt*, and it needs to be accounted for financially. Either an association can budget a certain amount toward bad debt each year, or it can wait until this category builds to unmanageable levels and then specially assess to recover the lost operating funds.

The last typical situation we'll describe here (though there are many others that we haven't mentioned) involves catastrophic failure of mechanical equipment. Sometimes, things just break. It may be the cooling tower or the boiler or even an elevator. In one brand-new condo, a rainstorm wiped out the electrical and mechanical system for an outdoor elevator, necessitating a $25,000 repair. That's a big-ticket item, and often those types of repairs must be made by special assessment. This example dispels the myth that new communities never have special assessments. That's simply not true. In fact, special assessments are perhaps *more* common in new developments, because the developer budgets are often so underestimated that the board has no option but to specially assess for shortfalls. Also, depending on the developer's response to various construction defects, it may be necessary for an association to correct these at their own expense and go after the developer later in court.

Because special assessments are . . . well, special, a special procedure is required to enact them. The Uniform Act doesn't address this issue, but it's likely that your state statute or documents do. Ordinarily, the board is required to consider a special assessment at a meeting that has been noticed for at least a couple of weeks, probably by regular mail rather than simply a posted notice on the bulletin board. Also, as a special assessment is intended for a specific purpose, many laws and documents specify that the collected funds may be used *only* for that purpose—or they must be returned to the owners. So you can't overassess for the cost of replacing your boiler, hoping to add an infusion of capital into your operating account.[3]

So what should your association do if it finds itself facing a budgetary shortfall? There are two or three options. The tidiest option is to simply amend the budget so that it accommodates the new financial realities, and to adjust everyone's maintenance accordingly. Depending on the type of community, however, the concept of raising maintenance midyear might be politically prohibitive. The second option is to specially assess for individual budget categories in which the association estimates there is going to be a shortfall. For example, the board could decide to charge owners for the total predicted cost of electricity or for the cost of insurance. This is sort of a backdoor way to overcollect money in an attempt to address a greater shortfall. Technically, it works, so legally it's probably OK. If you're concerned, call your lawyer. A third option, not always available, is to take out a commercial line of credit. This is a loan against assets (such as future assessments and lien rights) that would allow an association to make necessary repairs and then pay for the cost of those repairs over an extended period of time. A line of credit is a form of debt, however, so some associations may require owner approval before one is secured.

Once a special assessment is passed, it can be collected from residents just like a regular assessment. If you don't pay, the association will put a lien on your property and then foreclose, just as if you hadn't paid your maintenance. Which is yet another reason to get active in your community government—so that you can voice

---

3 In some states, any surplus from a special assessment can be rolled over into the operating account—but if there is money left over at the end of the year, it must be returned to the owners or applied as a credit against future maintenance. Also, associations must be mindful not to accumulate large amounts of unspent cash, because doing so might expose the association to tax liability.

your opinion on these important issues and be aware of them long before they arise, rather than getting blindsided by an unplanned and unexpected expense.

DELINQUENCIES

There is no SOC in existence where 100 percent of the owners pay their bills on time, every time. It just doesn't happen. Typically, at least 5 percent of the owners will fail to pay their monthly assessments for any given month, and it will be up to the association to collect the funds using the tools that the law provides.

Fortunately, the weapon that an association wields against delinquent assessments is one of the most powerful granted under the law: a *lien*. Basically, a lien is a legal right to hold on to another person's property until a debt has been paid. If you have a mortgage, there's essentially a lien on your property, held by the bank. If you don't pay your debt, the bank gets your house. In the context of this discussion, a lien is an association's legal right to record in the public records a charge against a unit until its debt has been paid. If your state has rewritten its laws in the past few years, the association may even have the power to file a lien not only for unpaid assessments but for *any* funds you owe, including fees, fines, charges for damage to common elements, or interest. Until that debt is satisfied, the unit owner will be unable to sell or refinance the property. If the debt isn't repaid within a certain amount of time, then the association can *foreclose*—take possession of the property. In truth, the law cannot grant an organization any stronger influence over a property owner. If you don't pay, it takes your unit to satisfy the debt; it is crucial to understand this. Liens are not optional, and they're not something to play around with.[4]

Of course, this power is meaningless unless the association is willing to both file a lien and foreclose on a unit. When the association forecloses, the property will be sold at auction on the steps of the courthouse, and the association may either allow it to be sold to a third party or bid on the property itself. Either way, the eventual purchaser will have to first pay the association's lien, and then the remainder of the purchase price goes to the original owner. But if an association is not willing to follow through to foreclosure, a lien is an empty threat, and it will be ignored by recalcitrant residents.

Because a lien is such a powerful sword, you can't swing it without first jumping through some very significant hurdles. Usually, the association must send a demand letter and then wait a number of days (thirty or more) to see if the owner pays the debt. Note that the Fair Debt Collection Practices Act, an extremely complex federal law that regulates debt collection procedures, prohibits communications from a debt collector that may be perceived as misleading by the debtor; for example, the demand letter must state the exact amount owed and must present arbitrary deadlines for repayment. Your association's attorney—the "debt collector" in this case—must be sure to follow the rules of the act strictly throughout this process.

If the deadlines have passed and the debt remains unpaid, then an attorney may file a lien against the property. The association must again wait a certain number of days to see if the debt is repaid before it can go ahead with the foreclosure. Throughout this entire process, the association may collect interest on the owed money, as

---

4 Some states have a law called a Homestead Act that protects homeowners against foreclosure. However, even in these states, an exception to the law exists when the unpaid funds were to have gone toward the betterment of the property. Courts have universally held that because association maintenance is used for upkeep and improvements, liens against assessments can always be foreclosed.

well as penalties (although it would be unwise to sit on a lien too long before foreclosing, as it may expire). If allowed in the documents, the association may also elect to accelerate future payments by the unit owner (requiring perhaps a one-year lump sum in advance). But all in all, the lien process takes at least a few months, and if foreclosure is required it can take up to a year.

Further, if an owner has been delinquent in paying maintenance, you can bet that he or she is also delinquent on mortgage payments—and the bank's right to foreclose will always supersede the association's. In many states, banks that foreclose are responsible for paying only a fraction of any unpaid assessments—so the majority of the debt will simply be wiped out and the association will never be able to collect.

The end result is that, while liens and foreclosures are very aggressive debt collection options, they do not ensure that an association will never have delinquencies. There are always some unit owners who would rather risk a lien on their property than pay their debts. When an SOC prepares the annual budget, it has to remember that a certain amount of that money will go uncollected, at least in the short term—and ultimately some amount of delinquency will never be repaid. This creates a cash-flow problem, so it's best to overbudget a bit in order to accommodate this reality.

In fact, when you break it down, there are really only two ways to prepare a budget: smaller maintenance payments versus stability in maintenance payments. Either you budget extremely lean and assume that a special assessment is likely in the event of any contingency, or you budget "fat" and assume the worst-case scenario will be that the association is left with a little extra money to roll into the next year. In your community, the lines will be drawn down the middle. And the only way to influence the outcome is to attend the finance committee meetings when the budget is being discussed and voice your opinion.

Other than lien and foreclosure, an association may be able to punish a delinquent owner by restricting his or her the voting rights. However, this depends on the specific state and even the type of property; in some states, for example, condos may not restrict the voting rights of a delinquent owner, but an HOA can. Some states can even allow an association to restrict a delinquent owner from renting out the unit, but that power would have to be specified in the documents. What the association can never do, no matter how appealing the concept, is restrict essential services. If owners are not up-to-date on their maintenance payments, the association can't sweat them out by turning off their air conditioners or stink them out by cutting their water. Even a frustrated community government has to let the owners live unimpeded while the legal process takes its course. Ultimately it's a rule that's designed to protect everyone.

SURPLUS

If the board has done its job properly and spent your money reasonably, there is at least some chance of surplus funds at the end of the year. The Uniform Act (along with most other states' laws) provides that this surplus must either be returned to owners in a lump sum or presented as a credit to the following year. Even if your state doesn't mandate this handling of surplus funds, however, the IRS probably does. IRS Revenue Ruling 70-604 states that if a cash surplus is neither returned to members nor applied to the following year's assessments, that money is treated as taxable income. Further complicating the issue, the IRS requires this choice to be made by the owners, not by the board of directors. So, technically, if an association has excess income at the end of a year, and if the membership at large does not vote to either return it to owners or roll it over, that surplus is taxable income.

In practice, however, the board of directors typically determines what to do with excess income, as directed by various state statutes. Of course, this raises a tricky question: Who gets the money? If a unit has changed hands, is it the prior owner who paid the special assessment or the current owner to whom he or she sold his unit? If a unit owner has paid thousands of dollars in legal fees to sue the developer and then sells the unit, does he or she benefit once the settlement funds are distributed? The ruling of the courts may seem unfair, but it's extremely simple, and ultimately it's fair *because* it's so simple: Money goes with the unit. Whoever is the current unit owner pays the bills, and whoever is the current unit owner gets any credits. That way the association doesn't have to keep track of every dollar that floats in and out or determine which funds are to be distributed to which prior owners, many of whom it may not even be able to contact. So if you are a prospective buyer of a unit, you should determine whether there are any unpaid assessments that you will have to assume.

What this also means is that, if you intend to sell your home, you should figure out any potential windfalls to the new owner and include those in your sale price. For example, if you know that a developer settlement will be released after your sale, and that it will amount to $10,000 in the new owner's pocket, make sure you charge an extra $10,000 for your unit. If you fail to do this, you can't complain later when you don't see the money. Now you know the rule, so either ignore it or take advantage of it—but don't rail about it later.

ACCOUNTANTS AND AUDITS

In addition to the everyday financial management provided by the property manger (and possibly the treasurer), many state laws or association documents require the association to provide various types of end-of-fiscal-year financial reports, to be circulated to all unit owners. (The fiscal year is almost always the calendar year, but it doesn't have to be.) Sometimes, the type of audit will differ depending on the size of the association; it would be inefficient to force a two-unit town home to pay thousands of dollars for an annual audit. But in larger buildings and communities, whether or not the law requires one, an audit is an extremely good idea. The board of directors should hire a trustworthy auditor to whom it can open up the books completely.

The reason for this is twofold: to protect the community from a representative who may be stealing funds from the association, and to protect the association from false accusations of stealing. The newspapers are replete with true stories of fraud, and there will always be unit owners who think the world is out to get them, too. An annual audit may be the only line of defense against a thieving manager, board member, or employee; most states will not investigate criminal complaints unless there is at least some evidence to back them up. On the flip side, an open and independent audit process will help to deter baseless claims of fraud by overexcited unit owners. If your association follows the rules, then board members will never have to worry about going to jail simply because a nutty neighbor calls the cops.

Whew! We made it through our discussion of money and finance. In summary, associations require money to operate, and the majority of these funds come from the members, usually through regular assessments. In every association there may be a few members who don't keep up with their obligations, and it will be the responsibility of the board to use tools like liens and foreclosures to collect what is due.

Next up, the chapter you've all been waiting for: the rules and regulations. What are they, how crazy are they allowed to be, and what happens if you ignore them entirely?

10 NOT IN MY CASTLE
(RULES AND REGULATIONS)

In general, Americans are not really "rules" people. In fact, one way of looking at the American Revolution is that it began in response to a dictatorial board of directors (the British parliament) that declared an unfair assessment (taxes) without listening to the will of the people (a membership vote). That negative reaction to authority has been an American tradition for hundreds of years.

Further, as we discussed way back in Chapter 1, there is a long-held belief that we should be absolutely unencumbered by external rules in our own homes. But the reality is this: As soon as a family broadens into a community, whether it's a commune, a condo, a city, or a country, rules become inevitable. Even the earliest human communities decided at some point that certain things weren't such a great idea—skewering your neighbor on the end of your spear, for instance—at least not if you're the one who ends up on the pointy end of the argument. In fact, when you boil it down, all rules are a form of conflict resolution. They're an attempt by society to provide a framework for avoiding disputes or resolving them without escalating to violence. The problem is, there are dozens of different theories about how to balance rules and whether to err on the side of fewer or greater restrictions. Every community is different, and consequently, so is every set of rules. You'll find SOCs with very few restrictions as well as those that tell you how early you're allowed to turn on the television. Different strokes for different folks.

The vast majority of rules are designed to regulate interaction between neighbors and to ensure that all can enjoy their property as undisturbed as possible. Rules designed to protect the common elements and prevent the deterioration of property values, however, make up a very important minority. These are the rules that govern how your shutters look or what you can do to your balcony. In general, every rule belongs to one of these two categories: avoiding conflict or protecting property. And some actually do both.

It's important to remember that rules are not optional. They're not optional for the board to enforce, and they're certainly not optional for owners or their guests to follow. Don't bring your potbellied pig or bobcat into a pet-restricted condominium, thinking, "They can't possibly care—who would say anything?" They *will* care. Arbitrators and judges are inundated with hundreds of cases on just these issues, and absent disability or other exceptions, the rule violator is going to lose practically every time. Rules and regulations are contractual covenants. They're not permissive, and they're not suggestions—they are terms that you constructively agreed to, in writing, when you bought your unit. That makes them fully enforceable, down to specific compliance. That is, if you finished your floors with $30,000 worth of Italian marble but your documents allow only carpet, a judge is not going to care one whit about your investment or the hardship you will incur by removing the tiles. You are going to have to remove them at your expense, under court order—no question. So again, to paraphrase a saying in the electronics industry, "RTFD: Read the (*cough, cough*) documents!"

Before we run through the most common rules and regulations that you'll find in an SOC, it's necessary to explain that the rules are separated into two classes, and these classes are treated very differently. For simplicity, they are referred to as Class I and Class II regulations.

A Class I regulation is a covenant, rule, or restriction that is written into the documents and recorded into the public record. This includes anything in the original documents as written by the developer, and it's safe to assume that this probably also includes any rules promulgated later by the board but also publicly recorded. Class I restrictions are clothed with a very strong presumption of validity, as owners have the opportunity to know about them before purchasing a property; if it's in the public record, you're assumed to know that it exists (remember constructive notice?). A Class I regulation will not be invalidated by a court unless the restriction is wholly arbitrary in its application, is in violation of public policy, or contradicts a fundamental constitutional right. The simplest example of an invalid Class I regulation would be a restriction against a particular race or religion buying into the community; this violates public policy, as well as various state and federal statutes. Another example might be a rule that gives the board the power, at its sole discretion and on a case-by-case basis, to regulate what unit owners wear on the common property (a case of arbitrary application). These types of rules will generally be invalidated if they are ever challenged in court, whether or not they have been recorded in the public register. But otherwise, Class I regulations are almost entirely bulletproof, so it's very important that any prospective SOC owner review the covenants, rules, and restrictions in the public record extremely carefully. If there's a rule that says no loud music on Tuesdays, it doesn't matter how odd or random that might appear—if there's *any* explanation for the rule, then it will be presumed to be valid and it may be enforced by the board. (In fact, as we've already discussed in Chapters 5 and 6, it really *must* be enforced by the board for the directors to satisfy their duty to the owners.)

Class II regulations are those rules that have been promulgated by the board over the years but never recorded publicly. The important thing to remember about these rules is that a court may invalidate them if they are unreasonable or if they circumvent a right granted or inferred from the recorded covenants, conditions, and restrictions. For example, assume that a board of directors wants to pass a rule that no pet snakes are allowed in a condominium. Living in the community is famed herpetologist Ssssimon Sssschwartz, and he has an entire menagerie of reptiles living in his home—including more than one hundred snakes. The board passes the regulation, and Simon sssssues.

If this had been a Class I restriction existing in the public record our friend Simon would be ssssscrewed. He would have to find new homes for all of his snakes—or a new condominium for himself. But as a Class II restriction, the court must first determine whether the rule is reasonable. Simon certainly wouldn't think so, but the test for reasonableness is only to determine whether the rule has some legitimate and explainable basis for existence. In this case, the board was worried that the snakes would escape, get into the walls, and breed, requiring a major and expensive eradication effort—and that's certainly enough of a basis to be deemed reasonable. For a rule to be found unreasonable it would have to have absolutely no basis in policy, and that's relatively rare.

However, there's another hurdle for the board to face: Does the rule circumvent a right granted or inferred from the recorded documents? The documents are silent on pets, which at first glance might seem to mean that the board is free and clear. But what it actually means is that, since there are no restrictions on pets, they are presumptively allowed. Assuming that they aren't illegal breeds, Simon has a right to keep the snakes in his home, and the board can't promulgate a rule restricting this preexisting right. Simon wins in court.

Assume, however, that the owners feel extremely strongly about this issue and decide to pass the rule by member vote, using whatever percentage is required to amend the documents. They still can't restrict those pets that Simon already has in the building. His snakes will be "grandfathered" into the rule, or permitted because the violation existed before the rule was initiated. As long as they're alive, Simon's snakes can stay. However, Simon will be prevented from replacing his snakes, and new owners will not be allowed to bring new snakes into the building. Of course, the grandfather provision can be very hard to enforce. What is to prevent Simon from clandestinely replacing his dead pets with lookalikes and claiming that they have never passed on? At least one pet lover has attempted to skirt the issue by purchasing a new poodle of identical size and weight, and even dyeing its hair to match the look of her original pet. People do crazy things for their animals.

There are a couple of defenses, however, that owners can raise to *lawfully* prevent an SOC from enforcing a rule: estoppel and selective enforcement. Here's how they work.

As a general principle, the law requires any rule to be enforced within a reasonable amount of time; otherwise, the violator may assume that the rule is not going to be applied. In the case of contractual covenants, this rule is called *estoppel* or *waiver*. In essence, if the board does not act in a timely manner to enforce a regulation, it will be *stopped* from doing so altogether. Take our friend Simon again. Assume that his condo *had* a no-pet restriction, and Simon was in the habit of walking his snakes every day, on dozens of tiny leashes, out in plain view on the property. Despite this, the board of directors failed to notify Simon that he was in violation of the community rules. If a significant amount of time has passed, when Simon is taken to court he is going to argue that the board is estopped from enforcing the rule, because he was openly violating it while the directors ignored it. And Simon is probably going to win the argument. The only way for an SOC to correct a situation where it has neglected a rule is to notify all owners, in writing, that from this point forward it intends to enforce the rule—but anyone who has been violating up until that point will be allowed to continue to do so. This is why it is critical for a board to enforce *every* rule and regulation, unless the directors are darned sure that they *never* want to enforce the rule (that is, that they are essentially abandoning it).

When a board of directors truly *doesn't* want to enforce a rule, this presents an interesting twist. A proposed amendment to the Uniform Act would allow boards to essentially "decriminalize" certain rules by officially stating that they will not be enforced for policy reasons. This would give boards a tool to fix unusually restrictive rules that were inserted into the documents by the developer or rendered unnecessary by changes in the community.

The second defense, *selective enforcement*, plays out exactly as it sounds. Just like our own government, an SOC cannot enforce a rule against one resident but intentionally ignore another similar violation. When Simon is taken to court, perhaps he can demonstrate that there's an eighth grader in the building with a pet turtle and that the board is aware of the violation but failed to enforce it.

If so, Simon is going to be allowed to keep his menagerie because the rule was enforced selectively rather than universally. It's a case of "what's good for the goose is good for the gander"; rules are to be applied either universally or not at all.

The wrinkles involved in community rules and regulations can actually be rather difficult for the majority of SOC owners to grasp. Society encourages cooperation and reasonable application of laws. "I know dogs have to be on a leash," a pet owner will say, "but not my dog! He's the best boy ever!" But that owner is going to be the same person who hits the roof when her dog is attacked by a less friendly animal that is also breaking the rules. Unit owners will plead for the board to "be reasonable," and often, because of the complex social interactions involved in SOC service, the directors relent. But wavering on rules opens the doors to valid claims of estoppel and selective enforcement, even when application of the rule might be extremely important to protect either the property or the residents. So, as difficult as it may be to accomplish, it's very important to enforce every rule, every time.

PRESCRIPTION PETS

Many people feel that pet ownership is a right granted them by the Creator and that the love of their "widdle cuddlekins" trumps any human relationship. On the other side of the debate are those who feel that animals are vermin, good only for eating or wearing; the concept of pet ownership disgusts those people no less than if their building were infested with rats. For the record, both authors are animal lovers who have owned multiple pets of different species and breeds; like many others, we fall somewhere in the middle of this pet-related sanity spectrum. But it is precisely this polarization that makes pet ownership such a contentious issue.

With apologies to the animal haters, it's important to realize that in our society pet ownership is the norm—and the courts recognize this fact. If the documents are silent as to whether pets are allowed, then they're allowed by presumption. Presumptively pet-friendly buildings—and in some areas of the country, these are the vast majority—range from highly restrictive (perhaps allowing only dogs, and then only under 15 pounds) to highly liberal (no restrictions on pets whatsoever, as long as various municipal zoning restrictions are met). It's amazing how common it is for buyers to ignore this fact, only to be horrified later by the pitter-patter of multiple little feet. If you can't stand the sight, sound, or smell of pets, then you should try to avoid living in a particular community unless it explicitly prevents pet ownership (though because of the Fair Housing Act, discussed later in this section, there may no longer be such a thing as a pet-free building). You shouldn't assume that such rules might be changed later. Moreover, even if an SOC has passed a rule preventing pet ownership, if that rule was passed after the documents were recorded it's possible that some pets were allowed to remain in the building because they were grandfathered in.

The problem is that pet rules are so broad and so difficult to enforce, they beg for abuse and selective enforcement. So let's run down some of the more typical rules and explain the ins and outs of their application.

If a building allows pets without any restrictive language, then it must be assumed that it allows all types of (legal) pets. A declaration can state that cats are allowed, but no dogs; however, if the declaration simply says pets are allowed, then the board cannot pass a rule stating that dogs are forbidden. Such a rule would need to be passed by the membership at large, and even then any preexisting dogs would be grandfathered. The same would apply to a host of other creepy-crawlies, such as rodents, reptiles, amphibians, and birds. Now, if a particular pet is prohibited by local or state laws, the SOC doesn't have to worry about explicitly preventing it, any more than it would have to pass a rule that no methamphetamine labs are allowed on the common elements. If keeping the pet breaks the law, call the cops. You can hear the gentle mewling of your neighbor's pet tiger? Don't call the board—call Animal Control. They will take care of the situation right quick.

However, the majority of communities have some kind of language regulating pets in some fashion. And it's not just the basic question of ownership. The most typical restrictions are pet type (say, cats, but no dogs), breed (dogs, but no pit bulls), weight (under 15 pounds), and location (not allowed in the common areas, or must be carried)—even temperament is an issue that may be debated by residents. Of course, conflicts arise from these rules, which can result in unusual consequences. It is not uncommon to see an 80-pound German Shepherd being hoisted through the lobby of a luxury condominium that allows dogs of any size but doesn't allow them to be walked through the common areas. To avoid trouble, resist feeding table scraps to your 14-pound dog until he eclipses the stated weight restriction, or the board may ask a judge to ban your pet from the building—even if that particular breed typically weighs only 12 pounds, and even if you've developed a canine weight-loss regime worthy of a prizefighter. If the pet doesn't make weight, beware the overzealous board member standing watch with a scale at the front door like a Soviet border-crossing guard.

In general, the manner in which these rules are policed will depend upon the culture of the building and the makeup of the board. There are pet-friendly communities and there are pet-unfriendly communities. Sure, the board is responsible for enforcing every rule—but boards, like all governments, have priorities, and it's not uncommon for particular rules to become essentially decriminalized. You should check with the property manager and the board to get a feel for the community's attitude toward pets.

Until recently, the basic issues involving pets revolved around simple calculations—are they allowed, what types, how heavy, and following what rules; and every owner or resident in an SOC was treated the same. That all changed with some creative application of the Fair Housing Act.

The Fair Housing Act (FHA) prohibits housing providers from discriminating against residents because of, among other things, "handicaps" (the actual term used by the FHA). Limb-related disabilities (such as paralysis) are the obvious example, but diseases such as emphysema or multiple sclerosis are also considered handicaps within the definitions of the FHA. Even mental and emotional problems, such as alcoholism or various neuroses or psychoses, can be considered so debilitating to basic life functions (e.g., eating, getting dressed, moving about) that they fall within the FHA's auspices. The term *handicap* is defined by another statute, the Americans with Disabilities Act (ADA), in a very broad manner, referring to a limited ability to perform such life activities as "caring for oneself, performing manual tasks, seeing, hearing, eating, sleeping, walking, standing, lifting, bending, speaking, breathing, learning, reading, concentrating, thinking, communicating and working."

But the FHA does not simply preach tolerance. The law also requires SOCs to make reasonable accommodations in rules, policies, practices, or services when necessary to give handicapped people equal opportunity to use and enjoy their property. The handicapped individual will often have to pay for any such modification, but this law has allowed equality of access by simple common-element modifications such as ramps, lifts, and landscaping changes (paving a grass easement, for example, so that it is wheelchair accessible). These modifications cannot unreasonably interfere with the rights of other unit owners, however. In one example, a handicapped woman wanted to lengthen the stairs in her pool to make access easier. However, the plans she submitted covered literally half the pool with a giant staircase, which clearly would ruin the pool for other swimmers.

The law also allows service animals (such as seeing-eye dogs) in any residential property, whether or not pets are normally allowed. You've seen the signs a million times: "No dogs allowed, except service animals." Now, it would take a stunningly curmudgeonly animal hater to deny a visually impaired person the right to a guide dog. However, for every sensible, judicious law there are thousands of disruptive types trying to find cunning ways to apply the law in a manner for which it wasn't intended—to their benefit. Such is the case with pet ownership.

Around a decade ago, a motivated but troubled pet lover made the following leap in logic: If handicapped people are allowed to have pets, why not just get "your doctor" (or your family member or friend who is a doctor) to write you a note that says you *need* your 5-pound Yorkie to help prevent a host of ailments? And just like that, the world of "prescription pets" (a term coined by one of the authors) was born. It is now in vogue to circumvent an SOC's pet restrictions by having a doctor write a lovely note detailing how the resident's mental and physical health would deteriorate without access to a kitty or a lap dog: "If I can't keep Captain Winkle in my new condominium, I'll be very sad and lonely (suffer debilitating depression), I'll be nervous at night (panic attacks), my aerobic health will suffer (dog-walking as necessary exercise)—heck, I'll be just as bad off as any blind or paralyzed person!" Never mind that such an argument is a fantastic insult to people who actually rely on service animals—for some, the "me generation" has lasted past the 1990s.

At first, judges were a little shocked by the argument, and the law took a few years to catch up with the "What about *my* needs?" trend. The courts have since developed rules to govern how one decides whether an animal is a necessary accommodation for a handicapped person—but those rules are now extremely liberal. First, the association needs to determine whether the person is truly "handicapped." People are considered handicapped if they

- have a physical or mental impairment that substantially limits one or more major life activities (including those in the ADA list mentioned earlier),
- have a record of having such impairment, or
- are regarded as having such impairment.

If you are thinking that this definition seems extremely broad, you are correct; it includes such conditions as diabetes, cancer, HIV, mental retardation, emotional illness, drug addiction, and alcoholism. Most of these diseases aren't immediately obvious, so the board may be entitled to request medical information to support the resident's disability claim. This is one of those areas where contractual restrictions trump privacy; if people want special treatment because they are handicapped, they're going to have to prove it. Now, if the handicap is obvious, thanks to the Health Insurance Portability and Accountability Act (HIPAA), the association can't go digging into your medical files. But it can ask for information to verify that the condition impairs one or more basic life functions.

The association's next step is to determine whether the accommodation (in this case, a pet) serves a specific need for the patient. And this is where disagreements can get extremely thorny. There's no real question that seeing-eye dogs are a reasonable accommodation to visually impaired people, as their assistance directly relates to improving the person's life function. The same goes for an animal trained to hear doorbells and fire alarms for the hearing impaired, or a dog trained to detect seizures for victims of stroke and epilepsy. The more difficult argument is proving, for example, that companion animals are a necessary accommodation to people suffering from depression, because they can't get through the day without the love of their dog. Over the past decade, this argument has been presented on hundreds of occasions, and various courts' responses have differed dramatically.

Originally, the trend in the United States was to require that any "accommodation" animal be individually trained for the benefit of the handicapped person. So a seeing-eye dog needed to go to guide dog school before it was qualified to help a visually impaired resident; just being an unusually smart dog wasn't enough. Today, while this is still the stated standard, the term *individually trained* has turned into a sinkhole. Has the dog been to an obedience class? Then it may qualify. In fact, a court in California ruled that it was a dog's innate canine qualities that made it a valid therapeutic accommodation—and that no special training was required.

If the courts continue in this direction, the rules governing handicaps and accommodation animals will become so broad that owning a pet within a pet-restricted property shouldn't be much of a problem for anyone with even a passing relationship with a doctor. The world of prescription pets is alive and well—it won't be long before you can go to your local pharmacy and order Fido in a bottle. Just make sure to open the cap before you get home.

RESTRICTIONS ON SALES AND LEASING

As we discuss throughout this book, one of the prime goals of any rule or regulation is to protect property values—and no rules have a more direct effect on property values than the various rules that govern whether you can transfer your ownership and at what price.

Before we begin, though, a note about cooperatives: None of the information in this section applies to them. As we discussed in Chapter 1, co-op ownership is not property ownership—it is corporate ownership. As such, the board of a co-op can generally restrict sales or leases. There is no legal concept stating that co-op owners should have a right to transfer their real property without restriction, because co-op owners don't own real property.

For the rest of us, however, property ownership carries with it a right of transfer that is almost always preeminent to all other rights. This right is called *alienation*, and it is basic to the concept of property. If you own property, you have to be allowed to sell it—with a few basic restrictions.

First, it is a universally accepted principle that an SOC can never entirely ban a resale. If your condo has a rule or covenant that allows a board to reject a sale outright, that rule is unenforceable (although, of course, an SOC *can* reject a purchaser who would clearly violate a rule in the documents, such as a no-pet condo blocking a prospective buyer who specifies that he or she owns pets). The framers of our Constitution were concerned with the protection of life, liberty, and property, and that includes the right to sell property that you no longer want, at whatever price makes you happy.

However, if there is an applicable rule or covenant in the documents, an SOC *can* apply a *right of first refusal* (or *preemptive right*), which we discussed in Chapter 8. While the exact language may vary, a right of first refusal will allow the association (or its designee) to purchase your unit at the same price and under the same terms at which it was offered to a bona fide buyer. Basically, if you have a buyer with a signed contract, you must first present that contract to the board of the association; it then has some amount of time (usually specified in the documents) before it must decide either to let the sale continue or to purchase the property. If the board does not respond, this is generally taken as an approval of the purchase.

In theory, a right of first refusal should have no negative effect on a seller—you've agreed to sell your property at a specific price, and the association is buying it at that price. However, the rule *does* prevent owners from selling their units to whomever they wish, and this can sometimes have frustrating consequences for the owner. But the rule also prevents a lot of chicanery—sales arranged for a friend or relative at a "sweetheart" price, below-market "short sales" (sales that take place at a price below the amount of mortgage debt on the unit), under-the-table payments, and even fraudulent sales for the purpose of securing illegal loans.

Even more important, the preemptive rule, if taken advantage of, will prevent property values from dropping below some minimum threshold (as determined by the board). For example, assume that the fair market price for a unit in your community is $400 per square foot. A seller in financial trouble arranges to dump his unit for the below-market price of $300 per square foot. This would effectively reduce the fair market value of your own unit—and all the units in the community—by bringing down the average unit price. So, rather than allowing that sale, the board itself would choose to purchase the unit at $300 per square foot and then resell it when the market has recovered. In the meantime, the association could rent the unit, bringing in enough profit to offset the lack of maintenance payments (since if the association owns the unit, it doesn't pay itself maintenance). A well-crafted right of first refusal can ensure that property values in an SOC are maintained at a market level and can prevent fire sales in tough times.

Though it seems fair enough, there are many property owners who become apoplectic at the thought of their association getting into the real estate market in any capacity, much less restricting the sale of their unit to their chosen buyer. However, this is an extremely shortsighted philosophy. Rights of first refusal, if properly applied, make everyone money in the long run by shoring up property values during difficult times and ensuring that, when you are ready to sell your home, you will get a fair market price.

Unlike sales, which cannot be restricted outright, leasing may be restricted and in fact banned altogether by SOCs, if this is allowed by the documents. Some state statutes prohibit retroactive leasing bans unless they are approved by the affected owner, but even these rules allow such bans to be applied against new owners. As with pet restrictions, however, if the original documents do not contain a ban against leasing, the board alone can't pass such a ban— and even if one is passed by the membership, owners who predate the ban will not be restricted from leasing their units (that is, they will benefit from a grandfather provision). However, once the original lease expires, no new lease or extension may be executed. Given that caveat, if the original documents include a covenant against leasing, it is quite enforceable.

Why would an association want to ban leases, restrict the length of a lease, or control how many leases can be entered into within a year? Transient populations are naturally difficult to control. New tenants are unaware of the culture of the community, and they are more likely than most to violate the rules and regulations, as they have no "skin in the game." Further, tenant violations are very difficult to enforce. Some associations have the power to evict tenants, but eviction proceedings take months, and by that time the violating resident may already have moved on. Other associations are relegated to seeking injunctive relief against the unit owner, asking a court to force the owner to remove the tenant.

Frequent short-term rentals also create a significant security risk, as it becomes impossible to know which residents should be allowed access and for how long. Finally, a building that is populated largely by transient renters is unattractive to banks, thus raising the cost of loans; such a property is consequently unattractive to potential owners, in turn lowering property values. It is therefore in the best interests of most properties to ensure that rentals are long-term (at least six months) and restricted to no more than one or two tenants a year.

A quick note about background checks: An association can only take actions allowed by the documents—so if the documents do not provide the association with the right to perform background checks, they can't be performed. Without the ability to restrict leasing, what would be the purpose? To identify prior criminals, sexual predators, or other "undesirables"? There are significant privacy considerations involved. Even if it had a right to perform background checks of new owners or renters, the association would not be entitled to then publish that information for other owners. So there are very few legitimate reasons for an association to screen residents. The issues of screenings, screening fees, and background checks should only become a valid concern of an association if it has a stated right to perform such checks, and if it has a specific purpose for doing so. Otherwise, leave the police work to the cops.

FAMILY UNITS

In nearly every SOC in existence, one primary concern of owners will be that each individual unit is treated as a home—not a boarding house or other communal property. The traditional way to ensure this is to define how many and what types of people may live in a unit—the "family." The problem, of course, is that the American definition of *family* has changed over time, as our society has become more tolerant of various "alternative" living arrangements. Yes, these include same-sex unions—but they would also include those young people who have not yet wed or older adult couples who, for financial reasons, are not interested in marrying.

Traditionally, the way to ensure that an SOC did not turn into a fraternity house was to include a regulation along the lines of the following statement (which is taken from an actual condominium document):

- Each residential unit shall be used as a single-family residence only.
- As used herein, *family* or words of similar import shall be deemed to include a spouse, children, parents, brothers, sisters, grandchildren, or a group of natural persons related to each other by blood or legally related to each other by marriage or adoption.

Twenty-five years ago this was a socially acceptable definition, although even then it would have discriminated against unmarried heterosexual couples. But most areas of the country have since recognized the right of unmarried adults to register together as a *family unit*, and modern antidiscrimination laws prevent SOCs from refusing to sell to people on the basis of their familial status. And while federal laws do not yet preclude discrimination against homosexuals, many state and local laws do. As state and federal law always trumps contract law (especially when it comes to civil rights), if this traditional definition of *family* is included in your documents, it's probably invalid. So unless you live in an extremely conservative state, you probably can't prevent unmarried couples from living in your community. [1] That doesn't mean that there are no options for a community that wishes to prevent high society from turning into skid row. Most zoning laws specify how many people may cohabit in a single room in a dwelling—and these local laws must be followed regardless of any language to the contrary in the documents. Often, only two people are allowed to live in a single room, so a three-bedroom unit can accommodate up to six residents. A disgruntled board can always pursue zoning violations, and these can be reported to local authorities as well.

---

1 Don't toss out the documents as a whole, however; accepted principle generally would require only that the conflicting section be ignored, while the rest of the provisions may remain in full force.

Also, while most SOCs can no longer discriminate against unmarried couples, rules may still require that a unit contain only a single familial unit *as defined by local laws*. That is, if your county allows people to register as a single housekeeping unit (or same-sex family, domestic partnership, or whatever the particular regulation requires), then your documents may state that only *one* of these family units may inhabit a single home. So while your association can't abridge rights that are granted by the government, it can insist that renters or owners abide by any applicable registration requirements.

Beware, however, as this type of restriction is ripe for abuse through the selective enforcement defense. If your municipality or state does allow antiquated language regarding the family unit, then that rule needs to be applied to all unmarried couples, whether they are straight or gay. An association can't ignore the older widower who lives with his "nurse" and at the same time kick out the married gay couple from Massachusetts. If you're going to discriminate, you must do so equally.

Restrictions on habitation also raise the issue of long-term guests. At the outset, owners should understand that having guests in your unit is really not a right—it's a privilege. If you have a frequent guest who is disruptive or damages the common property, the association may ultimately ban that person from visiting your home. Again, it's the difference between owning a detached, single-family home and co-owning property with your neighbors. When you own it together, everyone has a say. Many documents also will state that any guest who stays for over a certain period of time (say, a month) is defined as a renter and must therefore follow any rules that are applicable to renters. Such a rule prevents people from circumventing legal housing restrictions by overloading their unit with guests or stating that an unrelated adult is simply a guest of the family unit. This issue may never arise in a planned community in Middle America—but in coastal or resort vacation towns, it's very common for condominium units to become spring break getaways for college students and, it would appear, their entire dormitory. So the law does give the association power to ensure that the building is secure and that it is not treated as a flophouse.

MORTGAGE LIMITATIONS

As was explained in Chapter 9, the lifeblood of any community is the assessments that it collects from owners. It is therefore in the best interests of the association to ensure that owners have the financial ability to pay their bills. In a co-op, there's no problem—the board will simply reject anyone who it feels is not up to the task of keeping his or her unit and paying the maintenance. But condos and HOAs need to be more creative—they can't simply require that owners have a certain minimum income, as that would violate a host of housing and privacy laws.

What they can do, however, is restrict units from being mortgaged past a certain percentage of appraised value. This kind of restriction prevents owners from becoming involved in a heavily leveraged investment that they won't reasonably be able to support financially. It also ensures that, if an association needs to foreclose on a unit for nonpayment of maintenance, there is enough equity in the unit to make the foreclosure financially worthwhile.

SIGNS AND ASSEMBLY

In America we (the people) have a right to say whatever we want—correct? The Bill of Rights guarantees us freedom of the press and freedom of speech. Isn't it an inalienable right of all Americans to express themselves by hanging signs, passing out flyers, and being generally boisterous and vociferous? This is America, darn it! We know what you're thinking: "Why *can't* I hang a sign on my balcony supporting my choice for board president or encouraging my neighbors to recall a thieving director?"

The answer, of course, is that all the freedoms that we hold dear, all the rights that make America special, are rights granted to us by the *government*. This is a very important and wildly misunderstood distinction. The concept of freedom of speech does not mean that you have the right to say whatever you want about anybody, at any time and under any circumstances. It only means that the *government* cannot restrict that right (with some exceptions, of course, such as when speech is viewed as dangerous, or when the restriction stems from a reasonable "time, place, or manner" issue—feel free to enroll in law school for the details).

The right to free speech *can*, however, be restricted by private parties. Take, for example, a contract's confidentiality clause, which legally restricts what you can say publicly—and allows you to be sued for damages if you violate such a clause. Likewise, freedom of the press does not mean that you can publish anything you want without recourse, or that any periodical must carry your missive. It means that the *government* cannot restrict what is published. But private organizations, such as newspapers and magazines, regularly make decisions that information is not publishable, either because it is libelous or because the message simply doesn't fit with the publication's editorial viewpoint. Similarly, you will be liable for damages if you slander someone, even a board member, by making a false public statement that damages his or her reputation. There is no protection in our society for this type of communication.

This brings us to the issue of signage and assembly restrictions. Most SOC documents will include a rule or covenant stating that signs cannot be displayed on common property and may even include a rule that restricts certain types of solicitation (such as handing out flyers in the lobby). If this were a state or federal rule, it would be invalid because it restricts freedom of speech or the press. But covenants are contractual rules between private parties, and as such they can restrict practically anything. Of course, this explanation boils down years of doctoral-level legal training, and as such it is not very thorough. But for the intents and purposes of our readers—current and potential SOC association members—suffice it to say that, as a general rule, SOC rules that restrict signage or solicitation are valid and enforceable.

Except perhaps in New Jersey. This is where things get a bit tricky, with one or two rebellious states gumming up the works. As we discussed in Chapter 5, SOCs are a lot like miniature governments. They collect taxes, they police rules and regulations, they provide public services, and they have elected leaders who create policy. They even have a "contractual constitution," in the form of the documents. So one day, a judge suggested that if it looks like a government and talks like a government, it should follow the same rules as a government. For a brief time, SOCs in New Jersey were required to abide by similar "free speech" rules as their state and federal counterparts.

The lawsuit in the actual case was filed by a group of disgruntled homeowners who had created a community action committee. They were upset primarily by three policies. First, their New Jersey HOA had a rule, meant to reduce clutter, that unit owners could post only a single sign in their windows and a single sign outside their homes. Second, the plaintiffs objected to the association's clubroom policy, which included tiered use charges; they argued that the fees violated their right to freely associate. Finally, the plaintiffs argued that they were denied equal access to the association newsletter; they wanted the opportunity to print their own scathing rebuke of the association and its directors.

A trial judge applied a traditional legal test, determined that the restrictions were reasonable and enforceable, and held that an HOA is not a government. However, the appeals court reversed this finding, reasoning that the community *was* a "quasi-municipality" (that is, it acted like a city) and therefore must abide by special rules usually only applicable to governments (that is, the state constitution). This prevented the HOA from restricting speech, assembly, or publication of written materials.

The New Jersey Supreme Court ultimately overturned this ruling but acknowledged that the state has long recognized that, under certain circumstances, free speech protections may be extended to private property. In this case, it simply found (among other factors) that the original restrictions were reasonable "time, place, and manner" rules and were therefore enforceable. But this still means that in New Jersey (and perhaps California and Massachusetts, although there's not really enough case law yet to tell), an SOC may have to abide by at least some of the "free speech" rules required of state and federal governments.

This legal wrangling might be of interest only to lawyers or their budding apprentices. But it's hard to tell how far this state-action theory will expand in the future.

APPEARANCE, ADDITIONS, AND ALTERATIONS

Rules and regulations that govern additions and alterations to both privately and commonly owned property are pervasive—so pervasive that we devote Chapter 12 entirely to them. For now, just realize that there *are* architectural controls, and that their enforcement and passage work exactly the same as for any other covenant.

ENFORCEMENT

So we've described a number of typical rules and regulations, but there are literally thousands of variations—and all of them need to be enforced by the association. But how? The community can't put people in jail—that's a power reserved for *actual* governments. But it *can* apply fines—and in fact that's the most common form of punishment available. If you break a rule, the association can fine you, just as if you were getting a parking ticket. However, like a parking ticket, there are rules that the association must follow, including statutory requirements that look a lot like criminal due process.

Nearly every state has a statute that allows SOCs to levy fines against violating owners, and nearly every such statute requires some form of notice—an opportunity to be heard. This means that the association generally must notify owners of the violation and allow them to present their case in front of either the board of directors or an independent *grievance committee*. If your state statute doesn't specify how this should work, your documents almost certainly do. Often, to ensure fairness in the fining process, the grievance committee must be made up of a group of owners who are entirely independent of the board. Most states will also specify a maximum fine, typically around $100 per day, up to a total fine of $1,000 for a single violation.

Assume, for example, that Fanny McBottom is seen wearing a thong at the pool, a no-no at Evangelical Shores Golf Club and Condominium.[2] The association sends her a violation letter, informing her of the proposed fine and providing a date for a hearing in front of the independent fining committee. Fanny generally has the right to be represented by counsel at this meeting and to present a defense. Once she is heard, the committee determines whether or

2 If you think this story is far-fetched, check your documents; many have a regulation stating that "appropriate" swimwear (whatever that might be) must be worn at the pool—no matter how attractive the violator may be.

not to apply the fine and, if so, for what amount. Assuming that the committee agrees with the board's recommendation, it makes the fine official and adds it to Fanny's next maintenance bill.

But while fining is a straightforward procedure, collection is an entirely different matter. Some association documents allow fines to be collected with other assessments, and the association can therefore place a lien against the unit if the owner refuses to pay. Other documents require that fines be collected separately, and some state statutes prevent associations from placing a lien on a unit for unpaid fines. In truth, the rules are all over the map. If you can't assess unit owners for a fine, assume that the fine will have very little weight unless the association proves itself willing to sue the violator. Initiating a lawsuit is a ridiculously expensive solution, but sometimes you need to spend some money at the outset to ensure compliance down the road.

In addition to fines, an association may sue unit owners to require them to correct violations; for that matter, any unit owner may also sue another unit owner in order to enforce a covenant, and may recover costs and legal fees as well. Essentially, this is a lawsuit for breach of contract, and it asks for specific performance by the violator. For example, Evangelical Shores could get a court order stating that Fanny may not wear a bathing suit that covers less than two-thirds of her ample behind. Similarly, an association could sue an owner to force the removal of illegal flooring, repair damage to the common elements, remove an impermissible addition to the unit—really, anything that could be cured by actions rather than money. But again, lawsuits are extraordinarily expensive. Some boards, especially at smaller properties, may feel as though it's not worth policing their rules when the cost is so exorbitant. Remember, however, the all-or-none principle of estoppel—if the board ignores a rule, then it can't enforce it in the future, even if the later violation is more severe (and, presumably, worth more to the association to correct). It is a board's specific fiduciary duty to enforce the covenants and restrictions of the property, universally and to the fullest possible extent. So while fining procedures are often onerous, and while lawsuits are expensive, ignoring rules violators breaches the board's duty to the other members of the association and can prevent future boards from enforcing those rules. It's best to hit hard and early, in order to reduce future violations.

In summary, every association has a laundry list of rules and regulations that owners are required to follow, and these rules often govern areas of our lives that, in our homes, we generally consider to be sacrosanct. Typical rules will regulate pet ownership, sales and rentals, mortgage limitations, family units, signage, and changes in unit appearance. If a rule is violated, the board can enforce the rule using fining procedures that are established either in the documents or in the governing statute.

Our next chapter addresses one little rule that can have big consequences: the rule that governs *nuisance*. Something stinks, and it's probably your neighbor's cabbage. Can you do anything about it?

IT'S AN ILL WIND THAT BLOWS NO GOOD
(NUISANCE)

No use or practice shall be allowed that is a source of annoyance to residents or occupants of units or that interferes with the peaceful possession or proper use of the property by its residents or occupants.

This single sentence, present in some form in nearly every set of SOC documents ever written, has spawned millions of dollars worth of litigation involving individual unit owners, and certainly has been the source of a great amount of angst and vitriol. It defines the principle of *nuisance*—a word that has a very special meaning when applied to SOCs.

A nuisance is a noise, smell, or other bothersome condition or event that interferes with a neighbor's right of peaceful use and possession of his or her unit. The concept seems simple enough, but the definition is so broad that the conduct it regulates can be extensive. Smelly garbage might be a nuisance, but what about cooking smells? If you can hear your upstairs neighbors moving their dining room chairs across their hardwood floors, is that a nuisance? What if it happens in the middle of the night—would that change things? If your neighbors have friends over every night, and you can hear their door slamming open and shut when you're trying to sleep at 8:00 p.m., that would clearly bother you—but is it enough of a bother to allow the board to take action?

Because the concept of nuisance is so broad, courts across the country have developed a consistent set of guidelines that are used to determine whether an owner's activities are a nuisance to his or her neighbors or just a natural part of living in close proximity. Here's how it works.

The first part of the test is whether the bothersome event has reached a stage where it does in fact interfere with the resident's peace of mind. Traditionally, you have the right to be left alone on your own property—characterized by the expression "Live and let live." Even though SOCs are a hybrid form of property ownership, the law still attempts to provide owners with some of the same rights granted to other property owners—and the right of quiet enjoyment is paramount. But all sorts of things annoy people—so if this were the end of the test, practically every one of your neighbor's actions (and your own!) could be considered a nuisance. That's why this is only half of the equation.

The court will also judge on an important second principle: whether the incident in question would disturb a "reasonable person with ordinary sensibilities"—not someone who is hypersensitive. You may hate the smell of garlic, but that doesn't mean your pizza-making neighbor is infringing on the quiet enjoyment of your home. The court will not consider the effect the action has on people with delicate living habits, fastidious tastes, hair-trigger nerves, or unusual sensitivity to annoyance or disturbances. The question is whether an ordinary Joe would be so annoyed that the act prevents him from using his home "quietly." It seems like a pretty simple concept—except that there are a lot of people out there who are unusually nervous, fastidious, delicate, or sensitive, and of course they all believe that they are reasonable. This means that they are going to complain to the board over and over again about the same conduct, without ever letting up—ensuring that they become a considerable nuisance themselves. Some of these people even sue their neighbors, resulting in an overwhelming amount of expensive and unnecessary litigation.

While a test of "reasonableness" might seem vague, such tests are actually quite common within the law, because it is assumed that a jury of peers will be the final arbiter of any dispute—and if a dozen randomly chosen and disinterested people think something is reasonable, then it probably is. Just as we ask juries to determine whether they reasonably doubt the guilt of an alleged criminal or whether a business was reasonably careful in preventing injury to a patron, we ask whether a reasonable person would be annoyed by the actions of his or her neighbor. The thousands of similar nuisance cases that have already been decided, therefore, can help us to determine whether a jury would consider a specific action unreasonable. These published legal decisions provide some basic guidelines that cover some of the more traditional nuisances: smoke, smells, pests, noise, and criminal activity.

SMOKE

The question of secondhand smoke is not only pervasive within our society, but it is also extremely polarizing. Smokers feel quite strongly that they have a right to smoke in the privacy their own homes. Smoking tobacco products is still very much a legal activity. Bans smack of paternalism and, especially today, smokers are knowledgeable enough to realize that what they are doing harms their health. The typical smoker has made his or her own risk/ reward analysis and determined that the negatives of emphysema and cancer do not outweigh the positives of the smoking experience. Certainly, there are readers who can't fathom what the benefits of smoking might be—but there are an equal number who have just reached for another cigarette. Again, this is America; liberty is kind of our "thing." And freedom has to include the ability to make potentially harmful choices for yourself, including drinking, smoking, having unprotected sex, riding a scooter without a helmet, or driving long after your eyesight has faded.

The problem arises when those people who choose not to smoke are essentially forced to inhale so-called secondhand smoke (more accurately known as *environmental tobacco smoke*) flowing from their neighbor's vents. Smoke can present an actual, physical presence in a home—not only the smell, but also a visible element. Further, the smell can last for long periods of time in upholstery, drapery, clothing, and carpeting—making smoke a gift that keeps on giving.

Until about a decade ago, nonsmokers had very few rights when it came to avoiding secondhand cigarette smoke. It was perceived not as dangerous but as a normal environmental factor of everyday life. The first few times this issue was litigated, the outcomes were similar—the smell of a neighbor's cigarette was not enough to disturb a reasonable person, and so the hoarse pleas of nonsmokers were largely ignored. Of course, this was before nonsmoking ordinances became prevalent. As society has changed, so has the law. But a flood of "clean indoor air" acts have changed that perception, and today most people believe that nonsmokers do have a right to avoid environmental tobacco smoke. In most areas of the country it is now rare for smoking to be allowed in public buildings or restaurants.

Recent cases have recognized, at least hypothetically, that a large volume of smoke would potentially present a legitimate nuisance to a homeowner. Again, it's a question of reasonableness—as society changes, so does the benchmark for reason. Is the smoke so pervasive and unusual that reasonable people would feel it affects their right to enjoy their own home? If so, it is not inconceivable for a trial court to rule in favor of a nonsmoker. For example, in one case a neighbor's smoking was deemed unreasonable, but only when a *second* smoker moved into the residence. The double-barrel smoking generated so much smoke and scent that it effectively evicted the complaining neighbors from their apartment. Reasonable people don't expect nonsmokers to put up with a cloud of smoke in their living room.

A new fly in the ointment is the application of our old friend, the Fair Housing Act. In the last chapter we explained that the FHA requires associations to make reasonable accommodations for handicapped persons. People with emphysema or lung cancer could certainly argue that their disability requires them to be free from *all* environmental smoke—and, in the context of a rental apartment, some have done so successfully. It's not clear what accommodations are required of an SOC—they could be as simple as installing extra ventilation in a unit, or as severe as banning smoking from a building altogether. In the next few years, we're bound to find out.

So if you're a smoker, how do you protect your rights? The best way is to show some common courtesy for your neighbors and recognize that to a reasonable nonsmoker, smoke does not smell pleasant under any circumstances. Open your windows, install air filters, and make sure that any common vents are closed. The less your activity bothers others, the more likely it will be that your own right to do it is protected. Do what you want, as long as you don't hurt anyone else. That's a concise definition of libertarian philosophy, and it's nuisance in a nutshell.

SMELLS

Cigarette smoke stinks—but so do a lot of other things, including garbage, food, dead plant material, fecal matter, and urine. And all of these things can present a potential actionable nuisance.

Let's discuss food odor first, since it's one of the most common complaints. Cooking is a basic daily life function, and there is no law that controls stinky food. As our society has become more multicultural, complaints of this nature have become far more prevalent; eventually people are just going to have to realize that some annoyances are unavoidable in side-by-side living. Remember, to the Indian family next door, curry not only doesn't stink, but it's actually a pleasant smell—an intrinsic part of their everyday life. In fairness, they probably don't like your cabbage any more than you like their curry. And the smell of fish is pretty much universally reviled—but most of us tolerate it on a regular basis. Basically, you may not enjoy the smell of a certain food being cooked, but that doesn't mean that the cook is infringing on the quiet enjoyment of your unit.

So how do you deal with unpleasant cooking smells? Well, how about being friendly to your neighbors? Get yourself invited to dinner, and try the curry—you may learn to love it. Or you can casually mention the strong smell and ask if they could possibly turn on a vent while they cook. The simple act of being neighborly would solve 90 percent of all complaints between unit owners in all types of properties. If you can't tolerate unusual cooking smells, no matter what, then you shouldn't have moved into a co-op or condominium. Remember, it's not the right choice for very particular people. There are some annoyances that you just have to learn to deal with.

Now, cooking smells are quite different from food smells that are the result of unusual lifestyles or cultural practices. Let's say, for example, that your neighbor keeps dozens of herb boxes around her house—and that the olfactory effect of those herbs creates nasal anarchy. That might very well be an actionable nuisance—a reasonableness test would have to be applied. Does everyone in your community have a house o' herbs, or is it just the wacky fruitarian next door? These sorts of things can change the equation.

As we all know, once all that food is eaten, garbage accumulates—and garbage can make a *really* stinky mess. Some people take out their garbage every day, and some are so used to the smell that they can stand it for weeks. But unlike cooking smells, garbage is not considered a fact of life; it is not reasonable for your home to smell like a landfill. Reasonable people regularly take out their garbage and realize when their house smells. Besides the putrid odor, the health, safety, and welfare of residents all come into play. If there's a problem, you should absolutely report it to your board and insist that action is quickly taken. In some instances (depending upon the powers granted in the documents to the association) it may be necessary to get a court order to enter a unit and have the garbage cleared out.

This is especially the case if that garbage is being actively hoarded rather than just neglected. We touched upon the issue of hoarding in Chapter 5; hoarders are usually emotionally disturbed people who have an obsession with keeping *everything*. They hoard items in a belief that they are being frugal or that they might one day need them—or sometimes just because they feel an irrational discomfort when throwing them out. Some hoarders just keep clean trash (like paper and boxes), but many refuse to throw away actual refuse as well. Hoarding is a disease—a form of obsessive compulsive disorder (OCD)—which brings up the question: If hoarders are sick, couldn't they argue that they fall within the protection of the Fair Housing Act and that the condominium has to accommodate their hoarding? Surely we'll see a decision on this issue enter into case law before long.

The practice of "elder dumping" has created a subset of non-OCD hoarders, a generation of older persons who live alone but are entirely unable to care for themselves. Many of these people, too, do not throw away garbage, either because they suffer from senile dementia or because they do not have the physical ability to do so. In such a situation, the garbage builds up. To make matters worse, it is very common for elder hoarders to keep dirty adult diapers, which causes the smell to magnify exponentially. To some of you these descriptions will seem like whimsical fantasies, but there have been hundreds of cases just like these, especially in regions of the country where retirees are common.

Such cases have led a number of states to pass commitment laws; in California it's 5150, for example, and in Florida it's the Baker Act. These laws allow the police to put people who suffer from senile dementia or are mentally disturbed, and therefore unable to care for themselves, into protective custody to ensure that they do not present a danger to themselves or their community. As harsh as it may seem, sometimes an association has no choice but to contact the authorities and ask that a resident be committed. This happens in almost every retirement community at some point. If you're a board member, it's a tough decision to make, but remember that living in a fog, surrounded by filth, is not really a pleasant life for anyone, no matter how disassociated that person is from reality.

Elder dumping also creates other smelly nuisances that must be addressed by associations. Elderly people may be unable to care for their pets, and it's common for a pet owner who suffers from senile dementia to have a house full of animal feces and urine. Some older people also collect animals, especially cats—and the smell of a dozen soiled litter boxes can be overpowering. If your association doesn't limit the number of pets that may live in a single unit, your city almost certainly does; over a certain number, the unit technically becomes a kennel, and the pets can be removed by Animal Control.

PESTS

In addition to the unpleasant smells, the act of hoarding also brings up the issue of pests—rodents and insects. Garbage attracts both, as do mountains of boxes and paper. There is absolutely no question that mice, rats, and insects are an actionable nuisance, because they can be a dangerous health hazard. Reasonable people do not accept pests in their homes.

While smells are a nasty problem, they are also easy to cure— you remove the offensive object, and the smell goes away. But once bugs or rodents enter your property, it takes a professional exterminator and a lot of hard work to eradicate them. That's why it is crucial for SOCs, especially those where units are connected by common walls, to be vigilant about pest control by providing extermination services, either voluntarily or mandatorily. Make no mistake: Your association has the power to insist that an exterminator visit your home. You can argue that you oppose the use of poison or that you are sensitive to chemicals, but an active pest problem poses a great enough risk to the common elements (as well as to other owners) that an association may do whatever is necessary to protect the property—and the board can get a court order to force you to comply.

If you are concerned about poisons, try to work with the association, meet the exterminator, and discuss how the particular pest can be prevented with either environmentally friendly chemicals or unobtrusive placement. Modern exterminators will not soak your home in DDT; they may even consider alternative treatments such as boric acid or diatomaceous earth, both of which kill bugs but are harmless to people and pets. Roach baits can be placed under sinks and in other inaccessible areas, and knockdown poisons can be sprayed under cabinets and behind baseboards—where they kill bugs, not your family. But one way or another, your association has a legal duty to protect the property and your neighbors from the nuisance of pests.

Related to this issue of pests is the question of toxic mold. Mold is a fungus that grows in dark, hot, wet environments, particularly in humid Southern states; some types of mold are poisonous and can even be deadly. Once mold starts to grow, it can spread at exponential rates, jumping between units with alarming speed. So how does an association protect against mold? First, any hot-weather community should have a rule that any unit, whether occupied or not, must keep the air conditioner running continuously at around 76 degrees. Cold temperatures inhibit mold growth, and air conditioners naturally dehumidify the air. Second, any water leaks should be treated as true emergencies, and remediation experts should be brought in to dry out the furniture and drywall. Mold takes up to seventy-two hours to take hold, so quick treatment will usually prevent its spread. Infected drywall or wood must be physically removed and replaced, as mold-inhibiting paint is really not a great deterrent. Finally, if mold has taken up residence in a unit, the owner must be forced to correct the problem as soon as possible, and the association should carefully check any connecting units for damage. Careful prevention is the key to dealing with mold, because if it spreads throughout a building, the remediation costs often become astronomical.

So if your association demands access to your unit for the prevention or elimination of pests both large and small, you have no choice but to comply. Once again, it's just one of the rights you give up when living in a common interest community.

NOISE

Noise can certainly be a nuisance, but the range of typical complaints is so broad it may immobilize a board of directors. Some amount of noise is typical and expected in any high-rise or townhome community. Shared walls are *never* 100 percent soundproof. If your read your documents (and even your sales contract), you will most likely see a clause reminding purchasers that there is no such thing as a silent building. You can expect to hear a certain amount of noise emanating from stand pipes. You will probably hear the sound of the elevator going up and down the floors. You may even be able to hear your upstairs neighbors as they prepare for work or enjoy their weekly tap-dance lessons. So when is a noise normal, and when is it a nuisance?

Once again, this distinction depends upon whether a reasonable person would be disturbed by the noise, and whether it is the kind of noise that is typical in that type of property. Many years ago SOCs typically had very few guidelines for soundproofing floors between units. Most people had carpeted homes, and carpet is a great insulator—it muffles noises of all types. But since then, tile and stone floors have become popular, and these materials transmit noise much more readily. A 10-pound poodle's nails as he skitters across the room . . . high heels . . . sliding chairs . . . a basketball . . . even dropped candy, when amplified through a tile floor, may sound like an explosion downstairs. Today's SOCs have changed with the times, and most modern documents specify particular kinds of soundproofing for different flooring types. If it is doing its job properly, the association will keep not only records but also photographs of installed soundproofing and insulation.

So what if you're in a modern building, and your upstairs neighbor has installed the required soundproofing materials—but you're still bothered by the noise? You're probably oversensitive and therefore out of luck. You will always hear some noises coming from upstairs neighbors—if that's a problem, buy yourself a penthouse (or simply a detached house).

Perhaps, however, you live in an older, carpeted building, and new owners want to install modern flooring. This is where problems typically occur. First, given current guidelines, if your neighbors installed their floors without insulation of any kind, that's almost certainly unreasonable, regardless of any requirement in the documents. It is not unusual for homeowners to be forced to tear up an entire tile floor because they tried to save a few dollars on soundproofing. If you think there's a problem, have a sound engineer come into your house and record the loudness of various noises at different times. Above a certain decibel level, most courts will find the noise a nuisance; the exact loudness required will depend on the courts in your state. This calculation also depends on whether the particular noise is a typical household sound or something more unusual. The sound of footsteps can be expected, but the vibrating filter that powers your neighbor's thousand-gallon fish tank may be deemed unreasonable. Again, it all comes down to what's reasonable in your community. In rural Iowa, you probably can't complain if your neighbor's rooster crows at sun-up; in New York City, that would be much more of a problem.

This brings up the issue of noises that cannot be mitigated by soundproofing, such as barking dogs or loud music. First, your documents probably specify that no loud noises are allowed after a certain time at night. Second, most cities have very specific noise ordinances that prevent the same kinds of sounds. So if your neighbor is cranking heavy metal music at 1:00 a.m. and the association office is closed, then call the cops—they will treat the situation as a legitimate complaint. Just remember that you'll have to live with this person in the morning, so be sure you've really reached your limit before you involve the police.

Barking dogs are another matter entirely. Dogs bark—that's how they communicate. Like wolves, dogs are pack animals, used to being in groups—and their owners are the pack. When an owner leaves home, the dog doesn't understand that person will soon return; all it knows is that it's alone and not sure when it's going to eat again. Telling a dog not to bark is like telling a child to never, ever speak. It's not only unrealistic but also a little cruel. That said, a dog that barks all the time, just like a child that screams all the time, is a nuisance to any reasonable person.

So how much time is enough to be a nuisance? Consider whether the barking is intermittent or continuous, and how long it lasts. It's pretty typical behavior for a dog to bark for about a half hour in the mornings, after the owner has left for work, so in the past this has been found to not be a nuisance. That may be annoying to you, but the law doesn't consider whether *you* are annoyed, in particular. It looks to whether the sound would be annoying to an ordinary, reasonable person—and ordinary people understand that dogs often bark for a while when they've been left alone. If you want silence, live in a pet-restricted building (if you can find one—see our discussion in Chapter 10). Of course, if the dog barks continuously, that's not normal, and the noise would certainly bother any reasonable person. The balancing point is somewhere in the middle, and only a court can decide where it lies.

CRIMINAL ACTIVITY

While it may not seem to fit the typical definition of a nuisance, criminal activity can in fact fall within these types of regulations, and steps should be taken by any association to prevent this. For example—and many of you will be flabbergasted to hear this—it is not uncommon for prostitution rings to be uncovered in co-ops and condominiums (even in retirement communities!). While your first thought may be "Live and let live," remember that where there are prostitutes, there are pimps, and pimps tend to bring guns and other criminals. It is not cute when a prostitute, no matter how charming she may be, is using the apartment next door as a cozy hideaway for her johns. The same principle would apply to drug dealers, whether or not their clientele comprises a large percentage of the community. Dealing drugs is still illegal, and it presents a large security risk for any association. Whenever illegal activity is known to be going on, an association may not only fine the unit owner as presenting a nuisance, but may also get a permanent injunction against such activities and may even report the conduct to the police.

None of this suggests that the board, or any resident, should be advised to report every perceived violation of law to the association, or that the association should create a civilian police force tasked with narcing on nannies who enjoy a little bit of "glaucoma relief." You don't want residents searching the parking lot for expired tags or asking people they don't know for identification. Instead, the association should concentrate on activities that are true nuisances— those things that adversely affect the safety of the residents by degrading security and inviting unwanted strangers onto the property. Prostitution, drug dealing, illegal gambling operations,[1] and

---

1 A number of state statutes allow "penny ante" gambling in condominiums, as long as a single hand does not exceed some small amount (say, for example, $10).

child pornography would all qualify as nuisances to other residents, and they should be either prevented through lawsuits or reported to the police.

Generally, homeowners must avoid any activity that might be a nuisance to their neighbors by affecting the quiet enjoyment of their own property. However, an activity is only a nuisance if it would reasonably interfere with a person of ordinary sensibilities. Typical nuisances include environmental smoke, smells, pests, noise, and criminal activity.

Up next—architectural controls. Paint, plants, shutters, and screens. Who decides what changes you can make to the exterior of your property? Here's a hint: It may not be you.

THE MORE THINGS STAY THE SAME
(ARCHITECTURAL CONTROLS)

Up until this point in the book, HOA owners have sometimes said to themselves, "Whew! Thank God that's not me!" But architectural controls are the one area of regulation that is extremely prevalent in planned communities, and they have an even more dramatic effect on the lives of traditional homeowners than on people living in condos or co-ops.

Architectural controls are the grandparents of the various property value regulations. These are the rules that regulate appearance or restrict an owner's ability to alter or add to the unit. Conceptually, it is believed that an SOC with a consistent appearance is more inviting to owners and therefore supports a higher property value. Whether or not this is the case, most SOC documents contain at least some restrictions to ensure that the community has a consistent look, and that owners maintain their own property to a certain minimum level.

For example, we're sure every reader has driven into a townhouse community where every building is exactly the same shade of brown. Did you think every homeowner simply decided that exact shade was the perfect color for his or her home? No—the covenants of that community mandate that every building be painted in a specific color to maintain a uniform appearance. Maybe you've driven into a neighborhood filled with mansions and noticed that there wasn't a single hedge with a curve; that's because those particular HOA rules state that shrubbery must always follow a straight line or right angle. There are many thousands of these types of rules, all designed by developers and boards and many with the goal of increasing property values. Whether or not this is the case is an open question.

The most basic of architectural controls that you'll encounter are those that govern style, color, and landscaping. When your roof gets torn off by a tornado, can you replace the shingles with Spanish tiles? Exactly what color is Midcentury Yellow? And what about the shade trees that you were planning to put in your front lawn? Unlike the majority of SOC regulations, architectural controls often govern your conduct on property that you unquestionably own on an individual basis. As we've discussed before, this may seem to contradict the traditional idea of home ownership. But remember, these types of rules are contractual covenants, and there is no question that they are generally enforceable (provided that guidelines and standards for judgment are met).

Take, for example, Holly Huntington, famed historian and collector of antique statues. Holly lives in Houses Near a Lake, a planned development governed by an HOA, in a palatial mansion with four Corinthian columns and a couple of flying buttresses. Holly thinks that nothing would go better in her front yard than a few choice pieces from her collection: David holding a fig leaf, a cheery Buddha, and Cerberus, the three-headed dog of Hades. But the rules of the HOA are very specific: No decorative lawn ornaments may be placed in a manner that is visible from the street or that would otherwise detract from a neighbor's property. Regardless of whether this is a Class I or Class II covenant, it is going to be enforceable, and Holly will have to move David indoors. They're her statues, on her property, but that doesn't mean she has the right to do as she pleases. Holly lives in an SOC—and, as we've discussed at length, the perceived needs of the many outweigh those of the individual in this type of community. In fact, architectural controls have a lot in common with municipal zoning regulations, which is another reason that some people view SOCs as quasi-governmental.

Literally thousands of different types of architectural controls might be applied at various communities, and associations should not approve any owner's plan without reviewing it carefully. In one planned community, a homeowner submitted a plan to remove every single blade of grass from his lawn and to replace the lawn with white and blue rocks. The board approved the modification (evidently without reading the proposal) and then was horrified when it saw the final result. But when the board sued the owner to remove the rocks, the court ruled that it was estopped from doing so.

Here's another typical example. Until recently, it was common for communities to ban any decoration on exterior doorways, and those rules often included mezuzahs, crucifixes, and other decorative religious symbols. However, some states have since passed laws that prevent associations from barring the display of religious items on doorframes. In contrast, at least one federal court has ruled that an association may always enact such bans—so this is an area of law likely to be debated in the future.

Additions and modifications to property can also be governed, whether they are on limited common elements or owned elements. If your SOC rules say no pool decks, than you can't build a deck in your yard—that's just the way it is. This assumes, of course, that the rule in question is legitimate and passes applicable tests; the application of architectural controls, whether they are covenants or rules and regulations, follows the same principles discussed in Chapter 10.

Certainly, a board of directors should never tolerate unilateral modifications that affect the *safety* of the community. In an actual case, a pro football player decided to install a hot tub on his balcony, only to have the balcony collapse from the added weight, causing serious damage to the building. Even something seemingly benign, like a homeowner hanging his wind chime collection from the porch, can become a safety issue; in states where windstorms are common, wind chimes can very quickly become wind missiles, which clearly pose a risk to neighbors. Not every regulation is appropriate for every community, but each rule is usually a well-meaning attempt to solve some problem that has arisen in the past. No developer or board member sits down with a cackle and a twist of the mustache, wondering which random, onerous rule he can come up with next. You may not agree with the reason behind a rule, but there's almost always a reason, nevertheless.

Just like other rules and regulations, fines and lawsuits can be used to ensure compliance by owners. A court can also mandate that the modifying owners restore the property to its original condition, at their cost. That means if you tear down your shutters (a limited common element) to replace them with fashionable jalousies, you will have to not only eat the cost of your new shutters, but also pay to restore the building to its original condition. So before you make any modifications to your home, make sure you take a spin through your documents to see exactly what is allowed. Certain categories of rules are extremely common, and many of them have their own set of guidelines; we outline the major ones below.

FLAGS

With the renewed patriotism that followed the attacks on September 11, 2001, the idea of banning homeowners from flying an American flag from their homes has become unthinkable, although such regulations were once extremely common. In response to the attacks, a number of states passed laws that preempted SOC covenants and stated that a homeowner must be allowed to fly certain flags on certain holidays (such as an American flag on the Fourth of July, or a POW flag on Memorial Day). But in 2005, the federal government put forth the definitive word on flag waving. The Freedom to Display the American Flag Act states that an SOC may not adopt or enforce any policy or agreement that prevents a member of the association from displaying the flag of the United States on property that the member either owns or has exclusive use of (such as a limited common element). So while unit owners can't plant an American flag in the pool, generally they must be allowed to fly one from their balcony (in a condo or co-op) or from anywhere on their property in an HOA.

There are two limitations to this law. First, you still have to follow any federal rules that govern how a flag must be displayed. So if Congress ever manages to pass a flag-burning amendment, you won't be able to hang that burnt-out flag carcass from your porch. Second, associations may create reasonable time, place, and manner restrictions that are necessary to protect a substantial interest of the association. This means an association may create a rule that all flags must be mounted in a particular safe manner, or that they must be removed in the event of a tornado or hurricane. But, in general, this rule has removed any doubt as to every homeowner's right to proudly wave the red, white, and blue.

What about other types of flags, such as flags that display affiliation to an organization or group? Those can almost certainly be regulated, with one major caveat. As we discussed in the previous chapter, most courts have held that SOC associations are not governments, and therefore do not have to abide by constitutional rules like free speech. However, in those few states where communities are held to a stricter test, one could definitely argue that banning the display of any flag is a violation of free speech rights. You might wonder why you would care, but how would you feel if your neighbors hung a Nazi flag from their porch? Probably a little less generous about rules and regulations. This issue has not yet been directly dealt with by the courts, but if the cases in California and New Jersey continue in the current direction, we can expect that it will come up at some point, inciting a very interesting argument. In the meantime, you should assume that your association can't prevent you from flying an American flag (subject to safety restrictions), but that it can probably restrict any other type of flag or banner from being hung in any manner or location.

SATELLITE DISHES

There was a time not too long ago when satellite dishes were Buick-sized monstrosities, springing up from the backyards of homeowners like overfertilized portobello mushrooms. So it's not surprising that SOCs often regulated homeowners' ability to install satellite dishes in their homes, and especially in visible areas (such as the front yard or on the roof). However, modern satellite dishes are no bigger than an extra-large pizza, so they're pretty unobtrusive on any normal-sized home. In fact, the federal Telecommunications Act of 1996 prohibits SOCs from enforcing rules or regulations that prevent a homeowner from installing a satellite dish or antenna.[1] This rule is not absolute, however, and as always, there are exceptions in shared ownership communities.

First, because the law allows a satellite dish to be placed only on owned property or property to which the owner has exclusive-use rights, a homeowner cannot legally install a satellite dish on the outside wall of a condominium or on the roof of a multiple-unit building. Many homeowners believe, mistakenly, that they have an unfettered right to a satellite dish; that's just not the case.

Second, a condominium or cooperative can effectively co-opt this rule by providing a common-element dish to be used by all owners. If the building has a satellite system that you can access from your home, then you cannot install another dish on your balcony because, say, you'd prefer to use a different provider in order to watch your favorite shows. The administrative rules of the Telecommunications Act don't carve out an exception for alternative programming. An association that wants to protect the exterior appearance of the property only has to install a master dish on the roof, and it can continue to ban unit owners from installing their own antennas, even on limited common elements. If the condominium had only cable television, however, it would have no choice but to allow you install the dish. If this is an important issue for you as a homeowner, you should check the regulations in your community before you sign the contract, because the Telecommunications Act is not absolute.

---

1 Yes, this law governs antennas as well—those tall metal lightning rods everyone once used to use to receive television signals—though their numbers are dwindling, except in some areas of the country where cable television is not readily available and satellite service is simply too expensive.

BALCONY AND PATIO MODIFICATIONS

Balconies and patios are perhaps the most private of limited common elements; because access is generally only through the unit itself, these are perceived as being as close to an owned element as possible. However, "close" only counts in horseshoes and hand grenades. Often these structures are still limited common elements, and therefore they are still commonly owned.

The most common balcony/patio regulation regards appropriate flooring. There was a time when it was very common for unit owners to carpet their balconies, either with Astroturf or with regular household carpet. The problem, of course, is water retention. Carpeting holds water for so long that it allows the moisture to seep into the concrete structure of the balcony, weakening the reinforcement bars and leading to spalling (which then becomes a major, expensive repair). Most modern SOCs now require that balconies be finished with some form of tile, whether stone or ceramic. If yours doesn't, it should, because this is a collective responsibility. If a unit owner has an unfinished balcony and the concrete eventually degrades, the association may have to pay for the repairs.

Of course, this is separate from any appearance issues, which are also legitimate. Balconies can often be seen not only by other unit owners but also from the street; don't forget that the look of the building influences prospective buyers and directly affects your property value. Would you rather buy a unit in a building that looks like a luxury hotel or in one that has more exterior variation than a Shanghai flophouse? There is a visible and important difference between lax buildings, where owners can essentially use their balconies as storage areas for mops, bicycles, toys, and exercise equipment, and strictly regulated buildings where only furniture is permitted. You may prefer one or the other, but the type you choose will certainly affect your lifestyle and your unit's resale value.

It is not uncommon for unit owners to take it upon themselves to screen in their balconies, which, in an entirely unscreened community, can be a glaring variation. Some unit owners are simply ignorant of the rules, while some have no interest in following them—but ultimately their actions do affect other unit owners. And remember, the violating unit owner will eventually have to pay to remove the unapproved modification. So it's always best to check your documents and maybe even solicit your board for specific pre-approval of a project.

The last balcony issue involves hurricane shutters, a very common issue in storm-prone states. Florida is a bellwether for hurricane issues, and so its statutes governing shutters are very instructive. In Florida, every unit owner has a right to install hurricane shutters on his or her windows, notwithstanding any contrary provision in the documents. As always, though, there is an exception: The association, with the proper approval of a majority of unit owners, can choose to install shutters on *every* unit owner's windows as a collective project, the cost of which would be paid by the owners as a special assessment. (If this is option is chosen, then any owners who already have the proper shutters get credit for their portion of the special assessment.) However, once the association installs these shutters, it can then prevent the unit owner from removing or replacing them, as they are now a common element and to do so would be an unauthorized modification. So you may be allowed to install shutters but not to change ones already applied to your windows by the association.

The right to install shutters is rarely absolute, but it is becoming far more common, especially in coastal environments. If you feel you need protection, check your state statute and then your documents in order to determine your rights.

REVIEW BY COMMITTEE

In many communities, any modifications made to limited common elements and sometimes even individual units must be presented to the association; unit owners must address either the board of directors or an independent committee put together specifically for that purpose (generally known as an *architectural review committee*, or *ARC*). It is quite legal for your documents to require approval of these projects. However, there is a cardinal rule of law when assessing an ARC's scope of authority: The exercise of power by the ARC must be governed by the applicable covenants and guidelines and must be reasonably exercised, must be made in good faith, and must not be arbitrary and capricious. The committee can't deny your balcony flooring because the president doesn't like you, you don't pay your maintenance on time, or you have a noisy dog. The decision has to be consistent and rational, based on past decisions and a review of the modification's impact on the building. If you're trying to put down purple balcony tiles on an otherwise neutral building, the committee would have good reason to deny your request. But if the ARC has already allowed other unit owners to install variously colored tiles, it can't reject your proposal because you've chosen an ugly shade of purple. In addition, the ARC is not allowed to write new restrictive covenants or to cancel out or obliterate existing ones. So if your documents allow purple tiles, the architectural review committee can't decide to restrict them from your unit.

Rules governing architectural controls are perhaps the most prevalent and common regulations in any shared ownership community. An SOC is allowed to govern many characteristics of your unit, including its appearance, additions, and alterations as well as the placement of communications equipment such as satellite dishes.

Often, an architectural review committee will handle the approval process for any modifications.

Our next chapter addresses discrimination—when it's OK, and when it's not. You may be surprised at the answer.

THE OLD FOLKS AT HOME
(COMPLIANCE WITH HOUSING LAWS)

For those of us who were born after the 1960s, it is incredible to imagine that discrimination in the United States was once alive, well, and widely endorsed. As recently as forty or fifty years ago the general practice in America was that housing providers could choose to discriminate against buyers or renters for any reason. It was common for communities to prohibit blacks, Jews, or foreigners in an effort to maintain a homogenous enclave that purported to be protected from the perceived evils of society.

Then came the civil rights movement, perhaps the greatest and fastest mass social change in American history. By 1968, President Lyndon Johnson was signing the second Civil Rights Act, one important section of which was the Fair Housing Act. The FHA prohibited housing discrimination based on race (Asian/Caucasian), color (black/white), national origin (Irish/Polish), religion (Jewish/Catholic), or sex (male/female). In 1988, two more classes were added by amendment: familial status and disability.[1]

Taken in total, the FHA prevents both public and private housing providers[2] from denying housing to a wide variety of protected individuals and requires buildings to make modifications that allow for easier handicapped access. These days, everyone is used to seeing the handicapped stall in the bathroom, or the ramps leading into buildings—these and many more modifications can be traced to both the FHA and the Americans with Disabilities Act. Imagine for a moment that you are African-American, handicapped, and living in America in the 1950s. Not a pleasant world, by any stretch. It's quite a miracle that in fifty years our society has changed so dramatically (while our modern world is far from perfect when it comes to attitudes toward minorities, it's hard to argue that things haven't improved).

But this is only part of the story. In addition to the federal protections, a number of state and local governments have passed their own civil rights laws, which usually provide even greater protection to a larger group of individuals. Many local laws prohibit discrimination on the basis of sexual orientation, age, or political affiliation, in addition to the other traditional categories. Remember our hierarchy of laws: The community association is at the bottom of the

---

1 This revised act is sometimes referred to as the Fair Housing Amendments Act of 1988, or the FHAA.

2 The question of *why* these laws can apply to private individuals takes an advanced understanding of the commerce clause of the Constitution, and it has been debated by judges and lawyers for decades.

totem pole—it must abide by every law above it, from the municipal to the federal level. So start at the bottom, and work your way up.

As we discovered in our discussion of free speech in Chapter 10, the rights we take for granted aren't always as cut-and-dried as we remember from grade school. Nowhere in our nation's laws are American citizens guaranteed absolute and specific protection against discrimination of any sort. For example, a housing community *can* discriminate against any category of people who are *not* protected by law. In one Southern community, the documents state that the property shall never be "leased, sold, bequeathed, devised, or otherwise transferred . . . to any person or entity that may be described as being part of the Yankee race." It then defines a "Yankee" as any person born north of the Mason-Dixon Line, or even any person who has lived for more than a year above that line. While this restriction is unusual, and even offensive to some, it is not illegal under current laws, and it may be enforced. Also, discriminatory private organizations do still legally exist—in fact, they're specifically exempted from the Civil Rights Act. But the FHA is concerned specifically with mandating the equal practices of *housing* providers among all protected groups—and according to these guidelines, all SOCs must follow its regulations.

With all these rules and exceptions to the rules, the question then becomes: How exactly do federal, state, and local laws affect SOCs? Let's begin with a more detailed discussion of the FHA, and especially the rules that regulate housing for older persons.

HOUSING FOR OLDER PERSONS

First, let's start with a basic proposition: If your documents have a clause dictating that a protected class cannot live in your community, that clause is *void ab initio* ("invalid from the outset"). Now, that doesn't mean someone is going to jail—it just means that the rule is void and can't be enforced. An obvious example would be a rule that says all residents must be of this race or that religion—there is no situation in modern American society where such a housing proscription is OK (although an exception allows private religious organizations to provide housing for members of their religion). Depending on your documents, however, the invalid rule may not be so obvious. For example, many documents state that a unit may be occupied only by a single family, and then they go on to define a *family* as a group of people related by blood or marriage.[3] Such a description potentially violates municipal statutes that protect against discrimination based on marital status.

And what about children? Can't an adults-only community discriminate against children? And if so, what's the point of the familial status protection in the FHA? When familial status protection was first added to the FHA in 1988, it was intended to prevent rental communities from discriminating against families. It was not until the end of the congressional debate that this protection was extended to include other private communities. To counteract the obvious effect of this rule on adults-only communities, Congress added an exemption for housing for older persons. At the time, there were three types of adult communities:

- any community specifically designated to assist elderly persons by a state or federal program;
- any community intended for, and solely occupied by, persons sixty-two years of age or older; and
- any community intended and operated for occupancy by persons fifty-five years of age or older in which

---

3 These "family unit" statutes have a number of purposes, the most common of which is to protect the right of adult, unmarried couples to share their household expenses. For example, it is very common for older widows and widowers to choose not to remarry, although they live with a significant other as if they were married. These statutes also protect homosexual couples who wish to create a single home unit in states where same-sex marriage is not allowed.

- at least 80 percent of the occupied units are occupied by at least one person who is fifty-five years of age or older,
- the community has policies and procedures that show its intent to be housing for older persons, and
- the community has significant services and facilities designed to meet the physical and social needs of older persons.

It's that last prong that was a little sticky, and retirement communities were forced to hold AARP seminars and install shuffleboard courts in an effort to prove their dedication to a retirement lifestyle. In 1995 the last prong was removed, and today the housing-for-older-persons exemption requires only two things: that the community be specifically intended for older occupancy (a clause in the documents should suffice) and that 80 percent of the occupied units have at least one person fifty-five years or older living in them.

For the purposes of this book, we've ignored the sixty-two-and-older category because it's extremely rare to find a community without a single resident younger than sixty-two. Sometimes older people need a family member to move in with them and assist in their living (although true caregivers are exempted under the FHA), and most people want the power to bequeath their homes to their children. The vast majority of retirement communities are therefore of the fifty-five-and-older variety.

The important thing to remember, however, is that an SOC cannot just unilaterally decide to become housing for older persons. Such a restriction on alienation would certainly require the vote of, if not every single owner, a very large supermajority of unit owners. The requirement has to be stipulated in the documents, and it has to be very strictly enforced. As soon as the community drops below the 80 percent threshold, it loses its protection. Therefore, the community must have the right, in its covenants, to legally deny housing to people below the age of fifty-five.

In addition to allowing bequeathals to children, the 80 percent rule contemplates a situation in which one resident (usually a spouse) is above the age limit, and one is not, and the older resident dies. In such a case it would be unjust to compel the surviving resident to leave his or her home. But other than death, a fifty-five-and-older community must strictly enforce its age rules if it wants any chance of maintaining its status as housing for older persons. Of course, it is perfectly legal for an SOC designated as housing for older persons to require that no residents may be under age fifty-five, regardless of circumstances. Most, however, prefer to allow some flexibility.

There is another consequence, lesser known but extremely important, of the familial status protection granted by the FHA. As we've said, the association may not make any rule that discriminates against people on the basis of their familial status, including whether they have children. That doesn't only mean that the association can't ban children from living in the building—it also means that *no rule of any kind* can be discriminatory against children. The FHA's rule is extremely simple: It is unlawful to discriminate against any person in the provision of services or facilities on the basis of, among other categories, familial status. To the FHA, saying "No children in the pool" is identical to saying "No women in the pool." It may seem outrageous, but it's true, and it's been borne out by a number of federal lawsuits.

We know what you're about to say: "But I know dozens of condominiums where they don't allow children in the pool! Everybody does it—how can it be illegal?" Well, everybody does it, *and* it's illegal. SOC documents are filled with regulations that violate the FHA, although most are unaware of the proscription. Do your documents ban children from using the swimming pool? Invalid. What about banning kids from playing ball in the hallways? Invalid. But surely you must be able to insist that children be accompanied by an adult at all times, right? Probably also invalid. That's just the way some things work; there isn't a problem until there's a problem. Unless your community is designated as housing for older persons, if you ban children from your pool, one day a concerned parent may take offense and file an FHA complaint.

So what's an association to do if it wants to adhere to the law? The answer is relatively simple, but it takes a little creativity to implement: All rules and regulations must be completely age neutral. So whatever conduct you want to prevent, make sure you prevent *everyone* from engaging in that conduct. For example, instead of saying "Children may not bounce balls on the tennis court," simply implement the rule "No person may bounce balls on the tennis court." Or, instead of having a rule that *diaper-age children* are not allowed in the pool, modify it so that *no person who wears a diaper* is allowed in the pool. It's a minor change of phrase, but the second versions of these rules are perfectly legal, while the first are not. It's very important for SOC boards to consider these issues as they write new regulations and amend their old documents.

Of course, there is going to come a time when any board is confronted with a conflict—a rule that would protect the safety of residents but is also discriminatory. Take, for instance, the board of directors at the Strapping Young Lad Fitness Resort and Spa. This new planned development has a half-million-dollar exercise facility, complete with free weights and all sorts of other hand-smashing equipment. But it just isn't smart to allow children to use the equipment without adult supervision—and it is probably a bad idea to let very young children use the equipment at all. And in fact, Strapping Young Lad's insurance company is insisting that the community post a sign to the effect that no one under the age of sixteen is allowed to use the gym.

Fortunately, the courts have recognized that SOCs may promulgate discriminatory rules if they protect the safety and welfare of residents. So a rule that children cannot use the gym *while unsupervised* is legal, because it serves a legitimate purpose. A rule that children can never use the gym is probably not legal, however, because it is overbroad. Meanwhile, a rule that *very young children* cannot use the gym is most likely OK, because weight-bearing exercise is not considered safe for toddlers. In contrast, it cannot be argued that children cannot safely swim—so a rule banning children from the pool is going to get shot down if it is ever challenged. In contrast, an SOC could pass a rule that children under a certain age must be supervised in the pool—this is a legitimate restriction to prevent the well-known risk of drowning.

Overall, it's a balancing act, and there's no way to definitively say which rules are valid and which can be challenged. This is one of those situations in which a board will have to use its best judgment . . . and see what happens.

HOUSING FOR PEOPLE WITH DISABILITIES

We've dealt in Chapter 10 with most of the important issues regarding disability, but here's a quick review. The FHA prevents discrimination on the basis of handicap—which is loosely defined as a disease that impairs basic life activities. Remember that the law not only prevents discrimination but also requires SOCs to allow disabled persons to make reasonable accommodations or modifications to their unit and the common elements, if such modifications are necessary to provide them with an equal opportunity to use and enjoy the property. However, the disabled owner is generally responsible for the cost of these modifications. Modifications or accommodations may be as simple as allowing the owner to keep a service animal or as complex as building an access ramp into the pool. But whatever the modification or accommodation, it cannot be so onerous as to prevent other owners from enjoying the common element.

The housing laws in place today are not perfect, although the efforts made over the years to prevent discrimination are admirable. The problem is, certain regulations intended to protect one group can have unwanted effects on another. Consider the following example, which incorporates nuisance provisions, discrimination laws, *and* FHA regulations.

Silent Shadows, a townhome condominium complex, is officially registered as housing for older persons. The average age is seventy, and many of the residents are pushing the century mark. Their rules, designed to enhance the comfort of residents, are exceptionally strict: no loud noise, no cursing, no toys or balls allowed on the property, nothing with wheels permitted (other than wheelchairs or motorized scooters), and no unnecessary excitement.

Herman Ruhe, past president of the association, has passed away, and he has bequeathed his townhome to his grandson, Hector Ruhe. Hector is forty-seven, single, and looking for a new home. He doesn't care that most of his new neighbors are retired—he doesn't have much of a social life and keeps mostly to himself. Because Silent Shadows does not completely preclude residents under age fifty-five, Hector is allowed to move in, and the older unit owners view him with cautious optimism. After all, middle-aged people become "the elderly" soon enough.

Unfortunately, Hector is disabled, but not in a way that his neighbors would easily understand. He suffers from Tourette's syndrome—a life-affecting disease in which the sufferer is compelled to act out a number of ticks and rituals that often include loud cursing and inappropriate comments. Hector cannot prevent his uncontrollable outbursts, but he also doesn't want to become a recluse. So he sits at the far end of the pool, trying his best to stifle himself.

Hector's neighbors are $%&#*@! pissed. Their entire lifestyle relies on peace, quiet, and decorum, and now this young interloper has infected their common elements with filthy language and inappropriate behavior. Most of the residents are unsympathetic to his condition, as Tourette's syndrome is so unusual that people are often confused by the cause and its manifestation, and they don't really comprehend its uncontrollable nature. The board fines Hector for repeated offenses, and Hector sues.

Who wins this lawsuit? Must the association allow public cursing as an accommodation of Hector's disease, or is that accommodation such an imposition against other residents that it would restrain their own rightful use of the property? Remember, any accommodation made for a handicapped person must balance the needs of both parties. This is a tricky question, and there's no correct answer. Cases like this no-win situation have arisen, and the outcome is almost impossible to predict. That's part of the fun of being a lawyer (arguably, it's the only fun part of being a lawyer).

In summary, the Fair Housing Act is a federal law that prevents associations from restricting ownership according to certain protected classes, including those based on race, religion, and familial status. However, the FHA carves out an exception to this rule for communities that are specifically declared to be housing for older persons. Such housing must conform to certain regulations, the most important of which state that 80 percent of residents must be over fifty-five years of age. Overall, however, the FHA prevents discrimination against protected classes of people by ensuring that shared ownership communities remain open to all buyers.

Next up, risk management: When everything goes wrong, who holds the tab? Pay very close attention to your association's insurance policies, because ultimately it will be you.

NO RISK, NO REWARD
(RISK ASSESSMENT)

Since the beginning of time, our lives have been fraught with risks. Our ancestors huddled in dark huts during thunderstorms; we plot approaching hurricanes on grocery store maps. They ran from woolly mammoths; we lock our car doors the minute we enter a bad neighborhood. They battled fires with blankets and buckets; we keep fire extinguishers within arm's reach. We know that we will encounter risks in our lives, and so we assess those risks and calculate the best way to protect ourselves. That's risk assessment in a nutshell.

The first and most important element of risk assessment is *avoidance*. It is incumbent upon any board of directors, and indeed any property owner, to properly assess the risks inherent in the property and to take precautions that will reduce the likelihood of someone being injured (or a home being damaged) by that risk. Security precautions are an obvious example. We all know that the risk of theft or personal attack is an unfortunate consequence of modern life, so it might be prudent for a board to hire some form of security (especially at night) to help reduce this risk. The same analysis would go for storm shutters, fire sprinklers, fire extinguishers, and even life preservers at the pool. These are the precautions we take for risks that are not predictable but that are foreseeable.

There are also a host of very predictable risks, those that are caused by neglect or poor design. Imagine, for example, the risks inherent in having a public walkway that is strewn with vines. Any rational person could guess that someone might trip over those vines, and if it is the responsibility of the association to keep that area maintained, the association will also be responsible if someone gets injured. This type of risk can be mitigated by taking ordinary and reasonable steps to ensure that a property does not offer any obvious hazards. An uncovered well with no posted protection or warning would be a pretty traditional hazard, though it could be something far more benign—maybe a sprinkler head that is sticking up too far, or even a couple of tiles that have come loose. An association must make great efforts to identify potential hazards and then to take reasonable steps to prevent those hazards from becoming a danger to others.

What happens when we've tried our best, but the unthinkable still happens? The fire can't be put out, the storm is a direct hit, or the security guard came in just a bit too late? That's when insurance comes into play. Insurance is a game of chance—a legal gamble that appeals to even the most abstinent. You give a company a relatively small amount of money every year (relative to the protection you're receiving, that is), and in return the company promises to pay you a much larger sum if various events should occur. This insurance game extends to every aspect of our lives. We insure against disease and death, fire and flood, larceny and liability. We know that life has risks, and we've decided that insurance is one of the safest gambles we can make.

As we've described earlier, one of the primary responsibilities of any association is to maintain and protect the community. Essential to that protection is a duty to carry some form of insurance that guards against the catastrophic costs of various potential dangers and instances of carelessness. Many states require an SOC to carry hazard insurance at the very least, and most documents are even more expansive when it comes to describing the association's insurance responsibilities. In all, there are two principal categories of insurance: hazard and liability. Let's break them down in detail.

HAZARD INSURANCE

Hazard insurance, which is often called either *peril, casualty*, or *property insurance*, is insurance that protects the association against some type of damaging event. Any kind of destructive element can be considered a hazard; storms, fire, flood, war, acts of God, and acts of terrorism are all perils that may or may not be covered by various insurance policies. The key characteristic of a hazard, however, is that it has a chance of being catastrophic. If not, there would be no reason to insure against the damage.

There are two main types of hazard insurance: all peril and single peril. *All-peril policies* protect against any hazard, excepting a specific list of excluded items; for example, terrorist attacks are often excluded from all-peril policies. In storm-prone states, windstorms might be excluded as well. Ultimately this is a regional question, as the insurance offered in different areas will depend on the relative risk of the hazards particular to each area. *Single-peril policies* are those that protect against a single hazard such as a flood or windstorm. Windstorm insurance, also known as *hurricane insurance*, protects the property in the event of a hurricane, and it is mandatory in some storm-prone states. Flood insurance, which is primarily purchased through the National Flood Insurance Program, protects against the costs of damage due to rising water (especially tidal surges); it, too, may be mandatory for mortgage holders, depending on the location of their community (all federally backed mortgages in flood-prone areas must be protected by flood insurance).

The problem, of course, is that buying insurance is a gamble, and there will be some people in any community who do not believe in taking that gamble—at least not with their money. Further, buying insurance for an SOC is nothing like buying insurance for a private residence. When you buy homeowner's insurance, you will likely have half a dozen options, all offered by different brokers at different rates; comparison shopping will often get you the best possible deal. Not so with SOC insurance, especially in difficult-to-insure areas like coastal flood plains. In these instances, it is likely that only a single insurance company will offer insurance to the building or development, and the rates will often be chest-clutchingly high. Many SOC documents require the board of directors to protect the building for the entire "cost of repair or replacement"; yet a board faced with a mandate to purchase 100 percent coverage for the building will face loud and fierce opposition from uninformed residents who wonder why a better deal can't be found.

This is especially true of flood insurance, which, while prudent, is made optional by most laws and documents. As flood insurance is controlled almost entirely by the National Flood Insurance Program, a single provider with set rates, the maximum insurance that can be purchased is $250,000 per unit in a building, which is often far lower than the actual replacement value of a property. This discrepancy is compounded by the fact that insurance rates in flood-prone areas (such as beachfront condominiums) are astronomical; it's not unusual for a building to be quoted a $1 million annual premium. That's more than the total budget of many properties and as much as a quarter of the budget of even the most exclusive luxury development. As such, it can be an extremely hard sell, to owners as well as to the board. The best that some SOCs can hope for is to find flood insurance on the secondary market, through Lloyds of London or other insurer conglomerates. These policies will rarely be for full replacement value, however, and they are an imperfect solution at best.

The problem, of course, is that any insurance agent or attorney is going to advise his or her client to purchase as much insurance as possible—but the idea of paying a million-dollar premium is so impractical as to be nearly farcical. And so a very large percentage of coastal properties will remain insufficiently insured, with their inhabitants hoping that a catastrophic storm surge never tests their foundation. Some SOCs are even tempted to enter into insurance pools, a concept we touched on in Chapter 5. While some state governments now allow this unreliable practice, this effort to insure several associations offers no guarantee of sufficient repair or reimbursement—especially if all properties in the pool are hit with hazards in the same year. If the pool is ultimately drained of funds, the replenishment of that money will still come from the pockets of SOC members.

So if you are on a board of directors, you have some very tough decisions to make. First, if your documents or state statutes mandate the purchase of insurance, then the association must do so. Optional insurances, such as flood, raise tougher questions. On the one hand, it is always prudent to err on the side of greater protection; on the other hand, it is not reasonable to expect a property to spend a quarter or more of its budget on a single insurance policy. Combine this with the fact that an equal number of residents will vehemently object to expensive policies and fervently support them, and the board is faced with an issue that is serious, contentious, and guaranteed to create bad feelings. Like we said, it can be a thankless job.

LIABILITY INSURANCE

The second basic type of insurance protects against *liability*. This is the legal responsibility an association has due to carelessness, bad acts of employees, or accidents that occur on the property. When someone slips on a banana peel in the laundry room, or a stray dog eats a box in a storage room, or your building manager gets drunk and plows her way into a resident's parked car—liability insurance kicks in. Any time an association could be held legally liable for damages, liability insurance can swoop in to save the day.

The association has an expansive duty of care to protect residents and the property. First, every association has a duty to protect residents and guests from bad acts by third parties—essentially, to secure the property at a reasonable level so that criminal activity is discouraged. That doesn't mean that an association must be responsible for every criminal act within its auspices, but if the security guard is consistently sleeping on the job, and a thief sneaks into the garage and boosts a custom Escalade, there's going to be a serious liability problem. Second, the property must be kept safe. Any dangerous condition on the property—whether it be a hot electrical wire, a rake left in the grass, an open storm drain, or a slippery floor—is potentially a liability concern for the association. Because the association is responsible for maintaining the property, it also has a duty to reasonably protect against hazards. Any property owner is assumed to have *superior knowledge* of hazards on the property. If, therefore, the association does not use a reasonable amount of care to correct or warn against those hazards, it is said to be *negligent*, and the injured party can collect damages (unless unit owners in fact had knowledge of the hazard, in which case they simply failed to use a reasonable amount of care in protecting themselves). Negligence is the basis of almost every liability lawsuit. And who decides if the association has exercised reasonable care? A judge or jury.

Imagine, for example, bucolic Slippery Meadows, a planned community resplendent with lakes and marshlands. And alligators—lots of very large alligators, who also love luxury marshland properties, free from any dangers or predators. In fact, Slippery Meadows essentially invited the gators in when it reclaimed the land from the native swamp, and the gator population has thrived, munching on egrets and the occasional stray dog. These gators are an open secret among the residents. One board member, the association president, suggests that they post warning signs around the development, asking people to keep pets and small children away from marshy areas. But the rest of the board (and the residents) are adamantly opposed to this measure. They worry that the signs will reduce their property value, and that's one risk they're not willing to take. The president's suggestion is voted down, and the alligators remain Slippery Meadows's dirty little secret.

Then the Edisyns move into their new home. They come from Ohio, and they've never met a gator that wasn't in a zoo. So Stacey Edisyn has no concerns about letting her kindergartener, Joshua, play in the reeds by the edge of the lake, collecting snails. Alligators are ambush predators, and the gator comes out of the water so fast that Joshua can barely jump back in time. He avoids the bite but is severely terrorized. In fact, he is unable to go anywhere near water for the next year, and even stuffed gator toys send him into a screaming tizzy. Understandably, the Edisyns sue the association.

Cases like this are common, and they come down to the association's duty to protect the common elements, keep them safe, and warn residents against known hazards. In this case, it was almost certainly unreasonable for the association to fail to act on its knowledge of a significantly hazardous situation. In fact, choosing to *hide* the hazard to protect the bottom line means the owners will end up kicking in a much larger chunk of change when the Edisyns win a multimillion-dollar lawsuit. One can only hope that the association decided to carry liability insurance (which protects against exactly this kind of situation).

What about the board members who decided to ignore the danger to residents? It's very likely that they would be responsible, on a personal basis, for breaching their fiduciary duty to the other owners; recall from our discussions in Chapters 5 and 6 that directors are required to exercise their duty, despite whether the owners want them to do so. They can now be sued for a lot of money, and this is where another type of liability insurance kicks in: *directors and officers insurance*. A D&O policy protects against lawsuits for negligent acts by officers and directors, and as we said in Chapter 5, it's an absolute necessity for any association. Even if you follow every rule in existence, at some point an officer or director of an SOC is going to be accused of breaching his or her duty, and will likely be sued. It's just one of those things that are inevitable. Lawsuits are easy to file—there is no reasonable way for people to ensure that they will never be sued. Therefore it is a minor and very reasonable expense for board members to insist that the association protect them against that inevitability.

SOCs have a multitude of other duties, most of which will be covered by a good liability insurance policy. For example, a community that advertises round-the-clock security could very well be liable for a theft that occurs when a guard doesn't show up for work. And in one actual case, a guest of a resident broke his neck when he dove into a completely dry pool that was undergoing repairs. The few thousand dollars you'll spend on signs and barricades is nothing compared to the millions the association might lose in a negligence lawsuit. Any hazard that should reasonably be noticed and corrected by the association is a potential trigger for a lawsuit—which is why liability insurance, if not mandatory, is clearly advisable.

While hazard and liability are the two main categories of insurance, most associations carry a number of other policies. Boiler and machinery insurance covers damage to mechanical equipment, such as hot water heaters, generators, and elevators. Glass insurance is available as a separate policy for buildings where glass breakage is a significant expense. "Umbrella" policies are overarching cover-all policies that kick in when normal liability insurance runs out. A typical umbrella policy limit can be as high as $50 million—and a wrongful death lawsuit could eat that amount in one bite. Remember that an SOC is a commonly owned *business*, and it needs to be run like a business in every respect. That means protecting the property against lawsuits, both by taking reasonable precautions against injury and by insuring against the inevitable mistakes. That's proper business management, and that's the type of judgment that is expected of directors and officers.

Every community will encounter risk, and the board of directors must attempt to both avoid that risk (by careful management of the property) and ensure that, should an unforeseen disaster occur, the association is properly insured so that any damage can be repaired. Managing risk is perhaps the most important job of any officer or director, as the decisions made will directly affect the health and homes of all other unit owners.

We're rounding the home stretch! Our final chapter deals with termination—how to know when the association is dead, and where to bury the body.

THIS IS THE END
(TERMINATION)

They say that all good things must come to an end, and the same is sometimes true of SOCs. Whether by nature or neglect, there may come a time in the life of any community when it makes more sense to start fresh than to keep patching the holes in the dam. But don't be too upset. Decay is part of life, and the renewal that follows is essential to progress. You may not be alive to see it, but at some point your community is going to have to consider whether it's time to cut bait.

There are three main types of *termination*—termination due to economic waste or impossibility, automatic termination, and optional termination. Let's discuss each briefly.

The first type is often called *involuntary termination*, and it occurs when the cost of repairing or rebuilding a community is greater than the value of the property itself. Assume, for example, that a California condominium complex is hit by a raging wildfire. The buildings are so badly damaged that it would actually be more expensive to repair them than to simply tear down the entire community and rebuild it from the ground up. Or perhaps an older community has been so poorly maintained that the cost of upgrading all of the mechanical and safety systems (elevators, generators, compressors, and pumps) is prohibitive when compared to the raw land value. In both situations it makes more sense for the community to dissolve, sell off any commonly owned property and assets, and allow the owners to move on.

Automatic termination is similar, and it operates just how it sounds: A clause in the documents will state that, when more than a certain amount (usually around 50 percent) of the property is damaged, the association *automatically* dissolves. But these clauses should be carefully reviewed in disaster-prone areas, because they can sometimes lead to termination even when the owners would rather rebuild the community. Once the association is terminated, it becomes very difficult to collect the funds necessary to reconstruct the property.

Optional termination, in contrast, is rarely the only option for a community, but it is common when the market value of a neighborhood has risen so quickly that owners could easily upgrade if they sell their smaller, older project to make room for a larger, more modern development. Optional termination is also essential when

SOCs merge—by necessity, one or both associations must terminate in order to join forces.

In all three cases, the rules governing termination will be quite strict, because what we're really talking about is a majority of owners making a decision to sell the property of *all* the owners. That, of course, is a fairly extreme solution, so most states will have complex and precise rules that must be followed before a commonly owned community is dissolved.

Because state laws vary so dramatically on this issue, it's best to consider the rules contained in the Uniform Act, which treats both types of "member vote" termination (involuntary and optional) the same: Each requires an 80 percent vote of unit owners to succeed. Why not require 100 percent for something so drastic? As we've discussed throughout the book, achieving 100 percent agreement in an SOC is essentially impossible, and the laws recognize this reality. The 80 percent mark is itself extremely onerous and will only be realized when there is a real economic or practical need on the part of a community to dissolve itself.

If the community is able to secure the required vote, then the Uniform Act requires that the owners execute a termination agreement, which must be recorded with the local government. And that's about it! The common property is sold off, and the proceeds are distributed to owners based on the percentage of ownership. After that, all go their separate ways. Don't think of it as an end—it's a new beginning. Whichever developer buys the property will have an entirely new project designed in no time at all, which brings us right back to our first chapter. It's the circle of life—just a lot less important and with a little more shouting.

That's the end of our journey through shared ownership communities—the New Neighborhoods. We hope you've found it fun and informative. We're sure you've found you are now better prepared to deal with the daily quirks that are part of any community. Just keep this book in a stack with your documents and local statutes, and you'll be prepared to deal with any situation that could ever arise.

Good luck, and remember—be neighborly!

ADDITIONAL RESOURCES

Community Associations Institute, 225 Reinekers Lane, Suite 300, Alexandria, VA. 1-888-224-4321. Community Associations Press Online Bookstore. www.caionline.org/bookstore.cfm

> CAI is a national membership organization that represents homeowner and condominium associations, providing education, tools and resources to the homeowner leaders and professionals involved in the governance and management of shared ownership communities. Visit www.caionline.org for free downloads of *Rights & Responsibilities for Community Associations, Governance Guidelines for Community Associations* and other free resources.

Community Association Network. www.communityassociations.net

> The Community Associations Network is a public Internet resource for community associations and the people and firms who work with them. The site is a wealth of resources and information for officers, directors and unit owners.

Bickel, Brandon E., and D. Andrew Sirkin. *The Condominium Book for California*, 21st ed. (2009). Piedmont Press, 2200 Powell Street, Suite 990, Emeryville, CA 94608.

> Written for owners of houses, condominium units, townhouses, co-ops, or lots in planned communities in California, this updated 2009 guide covers member rights and responsibilities, association duties, elections, assessments, and disputes.

Cook, Rita. *Complete Guide to Robert's Rules of Order Made Easy: Everything You Need to Know Explained Simply* (2008). Atlantic Publishing Company, 1210 SW 23rd Place, Ocala, FL 34474, 1-800-814-1132, sales@atlantic-pub .com

Dunbar, Peter M. *The Condominium Concept: A Practical Guide for Officers, Owners, Realtors, Attorneys and Directors of Florida Condominiums,* 11th ed. (2008). Pineapple Press, Inc., P.O. Box 3899, Sarasota, FL 34230, www.pineapplepress.com

> A practical guide for operating a successful Florida condominium association.

Dunbar, Peter M., and Marc W. Dunbar. *The Homeowners Association Manual*, 5th ed. (2008). Pineapple Press, Inc., P.O. Box 3899, Sarasota, FL 34230, www.pineapplepress.com

> This manual provides a step-by-step explanation of the requirements for meetings, membership voting, and the necessary parliamentary procedures.

Florida Bar Continuing Legal Education. *Florida Condominium and Community Association Law* (2007). 651 East Jefferson Street. Tallahassee. FL 32399-2300, clebooks@flabar.org or LexisNexis, 1275 Broadway, Albany, NY 12204-2694, 1-800-833-9844, customer.support@lexisnexis.com

Galvin, Robert J., Ed. *Massachusetts Condominium Law* (2008). MCLE, Inc., Ten Winter Place, Boston, MA 02108, 1-800-966-6523 (fax 617-482-9498). Ref. # 08-013, Product # 1880134B00.

> This comprehensive resource offers guidance and recommendations on a wide range of condominium-related issues.

Hyatt, Wayne S. and Susan F. French. *Community Association Law: Cases and Materials in Common Interest Communities*, 2nd ed. (2008). Carolina Academic Press, 700 Kent Street, Durham, NC 27701, 919-489-7486, www.cap press.com
> This legal coursebook introduces students to shared ownership communities.

Jasper, Margaret C. *Co-ops and Condominiums: Your Rights and Obligations as an Owner* (2004). Legal Almanac Series. Oceana Publications, Inc., Oxford University Press, 198 Madison Avenue, NY 10016, 1-800-451-7556, custserv .us@oup.com
> This reference tool addresses the distinct differences and laws that apply to condominiums and co-ops.

Kuehnle, Kenton L., with Charles T. Williams. *Ohio Condominium Law* (2009). Thomson West, 1-800-344-5008.
> This handbook discusses a wide range of topics affecting condominium owners, condominium associations, and real estate practitioners, including the 2004 amendments to Ohio's condominium statute, along with the relevant Ohio Revised Code title and author-drafted forms and models.

Lorenzo, Vincent D. *New York Condominium and Cooperative Law*, 2nd ed. (2008). Thomson West, 1-800-344-5008.
> This volume analyzes and explains a wide range of issues surrounding ownership of a condominium or cooperative in New York.

Poliakoff, Gary A. *The Law of Condominium Operations* (2008). West Group. 1-800-344-5009, www.west.thomson.com
> Legal treatise examines state and federal condominium law affecting the day-to-day issues faced by practitioners.

State Bar of Wisconsin. *Wisconsin Condominium Law Handbook*, 3rd ed. (2006). P. O. Box 7158, Madison, WI 53707-7158, 1-800-728-7788.
> This handbook is primarily designed for attorneys who represent condominium developers and associations, unit sellers, and unit purchasers.

INDEX